A. Aileen M
Bre

August 26, 1948

Cotton in My Ears

Cotton in My Ears

BY FRANCES WARFIELD

1948

NEW YORK · The Viking Press

DECORATIONS BY EILEEN EVANS

Part of this book appeared in *The Saturday Evening Post* under the title "I Know What It Means to Be Deaf."

PRINTED IN U.S.A.

For Wrinkel

Cotton in My Ears

1

I GREW up in Missouri, in the suburbs of St. Louis, in a
household of two aunts and three older sisters. We were the
four poor rich Warfield girls — poor because we had no parents,
rich because our father had been a rich man and we lived in a
big white house with tall white Corinthian columns. We were
the wards of the St. Louis Trust Company and Aunt Harriet
and Aunt May were our guardians.

I was soft and soft-spoken, the beloved baby, the last one, the
little one, the poor little one who couldn't remember her
mother. I thought my mother had died long before I was born
— she must have, because everyone was so sorry for me. Actually,
she died when I was one year old. My father died when I was
four. I had no memory of him, either, but I associated him in
my mind with Old Mr. Bascomb, who had fought in the Civil
War and lived not far from our house at the Old Soldiers'
Home. Mr. Bascomb was a deaf man. He had been blind and

deaf ever since the Battle of Antietam. His face had a blank, vacant expression, and I had heard Aunt Harriet say Old Mr. Bascomb was so stone-deaf he might as well be dead. The words "dead" and "deaf" sounded very much alike to me. I was always getting the two of them mixed up.

Sitting on people's laps or on my special round needle-point footstool beside somebody's chair, I listened intently to grown-up conversation. Often I knew what the grownups were going to want and fetched it without waiting to be told. I came before I was called, sometimes answered questions before they were asked. This was to prove I was as smart and heard as perfectly as my sister Ann did, perhaps even more perfectly.

They called me a dear, sweet, lovely child, and I was. They also called me a funny little monkey, because I pronounced long words the way they sounded.

"Goodness gracious, I'm a radish!" I would exclaim.

It brought the house down. Where on earth did the funny little monkey get her words? Had I heard someone say, "I'm erratic," perhaps?

My oldest sister begged the aunts to let me come downstairs in my bathrobe and slippers and tell her newest beau I was a radish. My second sister wrote an English composition about my being a radish and brought it home from school marked "Excellent." My sister Ann said radishes were silly and made up funny mistakes of her own — reciting "Mary, Mary, white canary" whenever anybody was listening.

As long as the family laughed at me, that meant they liked me. It meant they hadn't discovered my secret and I was safe. I resolved to be very funny as well as very good until I was seven and my adenoids were taken out. After that I wouldn't be so good all the time. My sisters were constantly getting in and out of hot water; their lives seemed fuller than mine. When

I was seven and could hear the grass grow like everybody else I wouldn't need to be such an all-fired little angel.

I had a private hideaway behind some lilac bushes in a corner of our yard, where I pursued a secret ritual. Eyes closed, fingers in my ears, I would repeat the word "wrinkelstiltskin" seven times. It was a magic formula that was to help me hear the grass grow.

One day my sister Ann surprised me testing my magic: I was crouched in my hideaway with one ear pressed to the ground.

"What you doing — playing Indian? I'll play, too."

Ann was several years older than I was and had long thick black braids, whereas my hair was short and brown and too fine to amount to much. Ann knew a lot. As Indians, she instructed, we must keep an ear to the ground and spring up with wild war whoops when we heard the approaching hoofbeats of enemy palefaces. Later on I must be an enemy paleface, she said, and she, the Indian, would scalp what little hair I had right off my head.

When we had whooped and scalped a good while I brought the conversation around to the all-important subject.

"Can you hear the grass grow?" I asked, offhand.

"Oh, sure." Ann polished off a war whoop in mid-air and spun on her heels, her shiny braids swinging straight out from her head. "Can't you?"

Her live black eyes devilish, she dropped to the grass and held her head tipped sidewise, listening.

"Why, goodness gracious, anybody can hear the grass grow," she jeered. "Mean to say you can't?"

"I can hear it," I told her firmly. "I can hear it perfectly if I listen."

3

I mustn't let on I couldn't hear perfectly. People didn't like it. It made them scornful like Ann or exasperated like Aunt May and Aunt Harriet when they called and I didn't answer right away.

"She doesn't always answer when we call," Aunt Harriet had told our family doctor a few days before. "Do you think the child may not hear well? Do you think that attack of scarlet fever last year can have affected her hearing?"

"Doesn't answer, eh?" Dr. Benedict had given my ear an affectionate pinch and pulled his huge turnip watch from his pocket. "Maybe that depends on what they're calling her for. Suppose it's a whopping dish of chocolate ice cream — any trouble hearing about that?"

He held his watch a foot or so from my ear, and of course I said I heard the watch tick. I wasn't sure I heard it, but I would have sworn I heard hell's bells to please Dr. Benedict. He was such a nice man — big, rumble-throated, smelling like soap and harness leather; I dearly loved him and planned to marry him. A year before, when I'd been five and sick with scarlet fever, I'd hoped he was my father. But I knew better, now that I was six. My father was a dead man. I didn't know what dead was, except that some people were dead and gone. My mother and father were both dead and gone. They were not in our family any more. Possibly they had not been wanted in our family, for some good reason. Possibly they had something permanently the matter with them. Possibly they had been sent away for that reason.

"She hears all right if she listens." Dr. Benedict nodded. "How old is she — six? Well, let's see — suppose she's very, very good until she's seven. If she is, perhaps we'll take her adenoids out. How would you like that, Miss Cotton Ears? Once we get rid of those adenoids you'll be hearing the grass grow."

4

I must listen. The doctor said I could hear all right if I listened. But even if I didn't hear I must pretend I did. It wasn't nice not to hear. It wasn't polite. People didn't like it.

The doctor's watch was easy. It was like the approaching hoofbeats of enemy palefaces when Ann and I played Indian; I could pretend I heard that. Voices were harder because I was supposed to answer and do what they told me to do. Aunt Harriet was easier to hear than Aunt May. Aunt Harriet was tall and straight and formidable and white-haired and spoke sharply. Aunt May was round and rosy-faced and pleasant and her voice was too mild for comfort.

I must listen hard. Sometimes, when I didn't hear at first, it would flash over me, a second later, what had been said. I must never look blank. No matter how much I wanted to, I must never say "What?" "What?" was perilous. "What?" would give away my secret and I'd be exposed to deadly danger.

I could guess what would happen if Aunt Harriet and Aunt May found out the truth. If they made up their minds I really couldn't hear perfectly, they wouldn't want me. That was the deadly danger. They would have me called for by the Charity Guild wagon that stopped at the back door on Tuesdays if you sent word you had something to be called for.

"This child is imperfect," Aunt Harriet would explain to Aunt May. Perhaps she would simply write "For the Charity Guild" on a slip of paper, pin the paper to the collar of my dress, and set me out on the back porch steps.

Where would I be taken? To some poor family. Some poor tenement family that had to be satisfied with what children it could get. Or to an orphans' home. After all, I was a poor little orphan — everyone said so. Orphans were safe in our family if they were older, like my two older sisters, or knew a lot and had beautiful thick black braids, like my sister Ann, or were

5

dear, sweet, and lovely, like me. But a poor little orphan who couldn't hear the grass grow was on thin ice until she was seven and her adenoids were taken out.

It was a lucky thing my not hearing the grass grow was only temporary. If it were permanent, I'd have been sent away long ago. Naturally. A rich family like ours didn't keep people around who had anything permanently the matter with them. Why should they? I must listen until I was seven. I must repeat the magic word "wrinkelstiltskin" seven times every day, seven days every week. I must never let on to anyone — especially to my sister Ann, who might very well betray me — that I couldn't hear absolutely everything.

There was one thing I could hear that Ann couldn't. It was the sound of the ocean — a faint roaring in my ears that I got from a pale pink sea shell Mrs. George Furness brought Ann and me from the East, marked "Souvenir of Rye Beach, New Hampshire." "Hold it to your ear," Ann had directed. "You can hear the sound of the ocean."

Because the shell had come out of the ocean, Ann said, it had the sound of the ocean inside it forever after. I put it to my ear and I could hear the sound — a faint roaring that grew louder as I listened.

"I hear it," I said excitedly. "I hear it forever after!"

This was true. When I took the shell away I could still hear the roaring sound, in both my ears.

"Do you hear it forever after — do you?" I asked Ann. "Does everybody hear the ocean forever after who listens to the shell?"

Ann put the shell to her own ear. "They hear it forever after if they want to," she said. She took the shell away from her ear, and I could tell from her face she didn't hear the roaring

6

any more. "And if they don't," she decided, spinning around on her heels, "they don't care if they do or not."

Wrinkel came along at this time. I wanted a close friend. Also, in my world of aunts and sisters, a boy was interesting.

Wrinkel was invisible and inaudible, which left him free to do and say whatever he wanted. The first time he entered a room he found the exact center of the ceiling and drove in a large invisible staple. He tossed an invisible rope ladder through the staple, festooning it over the tops of pictures, curtain poles, and chandeliers, and climbed over people's heads, listening to their talk and making nonsense of it.

Wrinkel was smarter than anybody — smarter than my sister Ann. For one thing, he was a boy. For another thing, though he could hear as perfectly as Ann could, he didn't care whether he heard perfectly or not. He chose to hear, and to act on what he heard, strictly as he had a mind to.

No one ever jeered at a little boy like Wrinkel. If our cook ever asked him to gather about fifteen apples from under the tree in the yard and he gathered about fifty, Ann wouldn't make fun of him for gathering such a big pile. She'd know Wrinkel distinctly heard the cook ask for fifteen apples but decided, on his own, to gather about fifty. If Aunt Harriet ever sent Wrinkel to her room for the shears and he fetched shoes instead, Aunt Harriet would be respectful. She'd know Wrinkel preferred to fetch shoes, or fetched shoes for a joke; in any case, she'd know he knew all along it was shears he'd been sent for.

Wrinkel kept me safe from danger. When somebody said something to me and I didn't hear it, all I had to do was say, "Wrinkel, oh, Wrinkel, let down your hair!" I'd say it as fast as I could, running the words together. It didn't mean anything — that was the fun of it. When I said "Wrinkelohwrinkellet-

7

downyourhair!" it made the grownups laugh and call me a funny little monkey and the danger of exposure was averted.

When people talked and talked and Wrinkel didn't make sense of what they said, that wasn't because he didn't hear it. It was because he liked to make nonsense by weaving his own name in and out of their sentences.

"It gives me great pleasure to wrinkeluce Mrs. Wrinkel O'Wrinkelman." Thus the plump, breathy-voiced chairman of my aunts' Thursday Club, standing behind our big, heavily carved library table while I sat on my needle-point footstool beside Aunt Harriet's chair and Wrinkel climbed the chandelier. "Mrs. O'Wrinkelman has recently wrinkelurned from wrinkteen wrinks of wrissionary work in China."

In church on Sundays the invisible Wrinkel swung unconcernedly on his rope ladder and climbed in and out among the highest rafters, enduring the offertory anthem ("As the wrink panteth after the wrinkelbrook"), ignoring the prayers ("We have wrinked those wranks which we ought not to have wrunk"), giving scant heed to the long-winded sermon on the wrinketh chapter of the wrinkeleth verse of the Gospel according to St. Wrinkthew. Straddling the arch above the church doorway as the congregation filed out, he would mimic soundlessly and mock-solemnly, "Good wrinking, Miss Wrinkeldine — the wrinkatism's better, I hope?" "No better, Mr. Wrinker, but you're kind to wrinquire."

Wrinkel and I had a lot in common. Invisibility, for one thing. Mouse-quiet in a room full of chattering people, I often felt invisible. Then, too, I knew what it was to feel inaudible. Aunt Harriet sometimes told me rather sharply to speak up. I couldn't answer her back, because it wasn't polite, but Wrinkel could. If anyone ever told a little boy like Wrinkel to speak up he'd have jeered, "What's the matter — cotton in your ears?"

8

Those were the Seven Deadly Words: "What's the matter — cotton in your ears?" If anybody ever said those words to me, it would kill me. It would mean the whole world knew the secret thing about me, that I didn't always hear perfectly. That would be the end.

The deadly words were safe with Wrinkel. He'd never use them against a close friend like me. He'd use them only to kill the people he and I agreed on.

He killed people off for me all the time. He killed off all the ones I didn't like — the ones who cleared their throats pointedly or raised their voices at me, as if they thought I might not hear them. He killed off deadpans, when they mumbled some question at me. I'd mumble an answer and when they said the perilous "What?" — that was the signal for Wrinkel to kill them invisibly and inaudibly with the Seven Deadly Words. It was dangerous to kill people, but a little boy like Wrinkel could do it if he wanted to. He was invisible and inaudible; no one could kill him back.

I killed only one person myself, and that was Old Mr. Bascomb. I up and killed him on Memorial Day, at the gateway of the Old Soldiers' Home. He had ridden in the Memorial Day parade and looked proud and distinguished in his Civil War uniform and his hat with gold cord on it.

It took courage to walk past him all alone. My ears set up their sea-shell roaring, which always got louder when I was scared. I was terribly afraid of deaf people — they didn't like me; I couldn't talk loud enough; I was too shy. Moreover, I thought they might be on to my secret. I thought that, being deaf themselves, perhaps they could tell by looking at me I didn't always hear.

However, as I passed Old Mr. Bascomb that Memorial Day afternoon, I suddenly realized I didn't have to be afraid of him.

9

He was blind. He couldn't see me any more than he could hear me. He stood at the gateway of the Old Soldiers' Home, still wearing his uniform, smiling a little in the sun, and I stood looking up at him, wondering if he knew I was there. He didn't seem to. I was as invisible and inaudible as Wrinkel. It occurred to me to kill Old Mr. Bascomb off, because, as Aunt Harriet had said, he was so stone-deaf he might as well be dead — so I looked straight into his face and said, quite loud, "What's the matter — cotton in your ears?"

It was exciting, and perfectly safe. Old Mr. Bascomb's blank, vacant stare didn't change. He was a dead man. I had killed him with the Seven Deadly Words. I ran home feeling good. I felt exactly the way a little boy like Wrinkel would feel — strong and brave and full of secret glee.

I was so afraid of deaf people that I dreaded even walking past the old Nye place. It was a square, dark house — one of the biggest in town — at the end of a long avenue of locust trees. There were three deaf people there — Old Mrs. Nye and her daughters, Miss Eva Nye and Mrs. George Furness.

Everyone said Mrs. Furness was wonderful and bore her affliction bravely. And everyone said Mr. George Furness had the patience of a saint, going through life with his mouth glued to the end of his wife's ear trumpet. She had several trumpets — a tortoise-shell one and a silver one shaped like a coffee pot. (She put the spout in her ear.) Her favorite was a black one shaped like a hunting horn; it was dented and scratched and had traveled East to Rye Beach, New Hampshire, with her every summer for twenty years.

Mrs. Nye was so old and so deaf that an ear trumpet couldn't do her any good. Miss Eva wasn't as hard of hearing as her mother and sister, but everyone wished she'd give in and face reality and get an ear trumpet like Mrs. Furness instead of pretending like a silly ostrich that she could hear perfectly if people would only speak distinctly. Aunt May often laughed about the time she sold Miss Eva three tickets to a Charity Guild concert and had to pay for them out of her own pocket. Miss Eva understood her to say "free tickets" not "three tickets," and it was too hard to explain, especially since everyone knew that, for all their money, the Nyes were close and Miss Eva was sometimes suspected of using her deafness as a convenience.

When we were sent on errands to the Nye house I would try to make my sister Ann go up to the door while I waited at the gate. I don't know which of the three women I was most afraid of — Miss Eva, who snapped my head off for mumbling, or Mrs. Furness, who pointed her big black ear trumpet at me, or Mrs. Nye, who stared blankly no matter how hard I tried to shout. I guess I was most afraid of Mrs. Furness, though I was fascinated, at the same time, by her ear trumpet and the electric earphone in her pew in church.

I gathered that when Mrs. Furness put her hunting horn in her ear it made everything sound very loud; possibly it brought sounds from far away that other people couldn't hear. I wanted very much to put the horn in my own ear and find out what happened, though I wouldn't have wanted anyone to catch me doing it. I was always hoping Mrs. Furness would forget and leave it at our house so I could sneak a listen when nobody was looking, but she never did. However, I did once sneak a listen from the earphone she had in church.

I didn't know the earphone was attached to an electric amplifier and transmitter on the pulpit and that the rector switched it off and on. I assumed that, since Mrs. Furness kept this earphone in church, it was connected with God. One day, when

I was sent to look for a letter Aunt May thought she might have left in her hymnbook, I had a chance to try it out.

It felt sacrilegious to walk into the dim, empty church on a weekday and I held my breath with fear as I tiptoed to the Nye pew, lifted the earphone off its hook, and put it cautiously to my ear. I didn't hear anything except the sea shell roaring in my own ears, which always got louder when I was scared. The earphone wasn't working. God's earphones, apparently, worked on Sundays only.

As Dr. Benedict had ordered, I was very, very good until I was seven and my adenoids were taken out. Also, I pursued my secret magic ritual. Crouched in my hideaway behind the lilac bushes in the yard, I closed my eyes and put my fingers in my ears and repeated "wrinkelstiltskin" seven times every day. I even devised finer and fancier magic, such as avoiding cracks in the pavement and touching every other railing of every fence I ever passed.

"Can you hear now?" my sister Ann wanted to know, as soon as my adenoids had been taken out. "Can you hear perfectly?"

I nodded. My throat was too sore for me to say anything. I was sitting up in bed with an ice collar around my neck eating cracked ice out of a bowl. Nothing had happened. Instead of feeling keen as an Indian brave's, my hearing felt as usual, cottony around the edges. But naturally I wasn't letting on to Ann.

"I bet you can't," she said. "I bet you're deaf. I bet you're deaf."

She swung her braids and spun around on her heels. I wished Wrinkel were there. If Wrinkel had been there, he would have killed Ann off for me.

2

LIKE most children who are about to start school, I felt that I was the most important one in our family and probably the most important in the world.

"Here comes the last one," Judge Hopkins would say, when I went with my three sisters to the St. Louis Trust Company to see him. He would swing around in his swivel chair and hold out both arms to me — a big, smiling man with even white teeth and a thick walrus mustache. He was president of the Trust Company and had been my father's great friend.

"Here comes the last one." He would lift me onto his wide, solid knee and I'd sit there, proud in my stylish linen Peter Thompson suit and round hat with an elastic band under my chin. "Here comes the last one and the least one."

It was the Judge's joke, about my being the least one. I wasn't the least one. Enthroned on his knee, I'd protest securely, "I'm not the least one. I'm the best one."

"The best one, are you? Well, that's different." The Judge would open a drawer in his big roll-top desk and take out a penny for me — a new-minted penny no one else had ever had. "In that case," he would say, eyeing me judicially, as a Judge should — "In that case it is the opinion of this Court that a penny is not one cent too much."

I was in love with Judge Hopkins and planned to marry him. It was his own idea. He was a bachelor and when anyone asked him why he didn't marry he said he was waiting for me. I had a collection of new pennies he had given me. I was saving them to discover electricity with.

There was a park in St. Louis that had the usual statues of famous people, and I felt sure that eventually there would be a statue of me there. One of the biggest was a life-size statue of Benjamin Franklin, and I had it in mind to discover electricity, because that was what he had done, and you didn't need anything but a key tied to the tail of a kite to do it. I planned to use the Judge's new-minted pennies instead of a key; being so shiny they'd surely attract lightning. Besides, Aunt May and Aunt Harriet were fussy about keys, though I could swipe a key if necessary. The thing was to have my statue in the park. In addition, once I'd discovered electricity I'd be able to hear perfectly.

I wanted perfect hearing by the day after Labor Day, when I was to start school. I'd need good ears for school. Suppose — my heart thumped in panic — suppose a teacher were to put me on the front seat and raise her voice when she spoke to me. If that happened, I'd be queer. The other children would call me Tin Ear. They wouldn't like me. No one would associate with me. Why should anyone? Nobody associated with queer children. I certainly didn't, myself.

Luckily when my kite was struck by lightning it would re-

14

store my hearing. I knew that, because Aunt Harriet had read a newspaper story aloud to Aunt May about a woman who had been sitting beside an open window during an electrical storm with a pair of scissors in her hand. Lightning had struck the scissors. According to the newspaper story, the woman had been somewhat deaf, but when her scissors were struck by lightning her hearing was restored.

It was a wonder, Aunt May gasped, that the woman hadn't been killed — and that was what kept me postponing my own discovery of electricity, though I had kites on hand and plenty of Judge Hopkins' pennies and Labor Day was not far off. Then a big electrical storm came up. Lights were out and wires down all over town and the next day we heard that a little girl named Alice Hart had been electrocuted by touching a live wire that had fallen in her yard.

"Just imagine," my best friend, Pamela Jones, said to me, the day after the big storm. "Alice Hart is at the funeral parlor, laid out in her coffin."

Pamela's usually rowdy voice was mysterious and quiet. There was mysterious excitement on her freckled, pug-nosed face. "Don't tell anybody — we'll sneak off," she said. "We don't want to miss it. Judas Priest, just imagine us missing a thing like that."

We walked downtown together, stepping over puddles and fallen branches of trees that still littered the pavement. When we got to the funeral parlor on Main Street, Pamela took me by the hand.

It was dim inside the funeral parlor. At first I didn't see Alice; all I saw was a lot of flowers. Then I saw Alice's head and shoulders lying in a white coffin.

I knew Alice. You knew all the children your own age in a

15

suburban town like ours, whether they went to your school and Sunday school or not. Alice was a pale girl with straight ash-blond hair and very pale eyelashes. Her father owned the jewelry store on Main Street and I had often seen her sitting beside him on a high stool behind the counter. He let her touch things and screw his magnifying glass in her eye, and I envied her the way I always envied children whose fathers owned stores and let them go behind the counters and touch things.

In her coffin, which was padded with light-blue silk just like the jewel cases in Mr. Hart's window, Alice looked paler than ever. Her eyes were closed and she seemed blind. Her eyelids and her whole face were bluish-white and luminous, as if she were made of milk glass, like the milk-glass hen we had in a china cabinet at home.

"Is she dead?" I asked Pamela.

I didn't hear Pamela answer. I was staring at Alice Hart. Her blank, vacant expression reminded me of Old Mr. Bas-comb, the time I killed him at the gateway of the Old Soldiers' Home.

"Is Alice dead?" I asked again.

"Judas Priest, pipe down. Of course she's dead. Just imagine being electrocuted and not being dead. Judas Priest!"

Pamela was scared, I could tell. Her hand was cold and her freckles stood out clearly. It was a sign she was scared, too, when she said "Judas Priest" recklessly. That was a masculine expression we'd picked up from the man my oldest sister was engaged to marry. We were careful of it and didn't use it recklessly.

I was good and scared myself. I knew I had no business being in the funeral parlor. Aunt May and Aunt Harriet would never have allowed it. They would have blamed Pamela. They didn't think too highly of her, though naturally she and I were best

16

friends. The Joneses lived next door to us and went to our church and Pamela and I were both seven and would enter Dean Academy together. Aunt May and Aunt Harriet said Pamela was a rowdy wild Indian. They said she talked too loud for a little girl and used unladylike expressions like "golly" and "gosh." They'd have had a fit if they'd known she said "Judas Priest."

Pamela pulled at me urgently. "Come on. Judas Priest, can't you stop staring and come on?"

I gave up my idea of discovering electricity after that. It seemed ticklish, because it was obvious that, while electricity could make you famous like Benjamin Franklin and restore you to perfect hearing like the woman with the scissors, it could also electrocute you.

I decided it didn't matter whether I discovered electricity or not. There'd be a life-size statue of me in the park someday in any case. And I'd soon be able to hear perfectly. Dr. Benedict said if I took iron tonic and stopped having head colds long enough to give my Eustachian tubes a chance to clear up I'd be all right in a year or so. It wasn't as if there were anything permanently the matter with my hearing.

All I'd have to do when I started at Dean Academy the day after Labor Day was to remember two things. First, to be very bright, so the teacher would think I heard everything she said. Second, to be very nice, so everybody would like me and never dream there was anything even temporarily the matter with me.

In class I paid close attention, my eyes on the teacher's face. I learned my textbooks by heart. When I was sure of the question, I volunteered to recite. My written work was perfect, my report card a garden of A's.

Teachers called me a nice bright child. Children called me Prissy because I sat up straight and kept my eyes front. They called me Teacher's Pet because I wouldn't whisper behind my geography book. (I would have whispered but too often I wasn't sure what they were whispering about.) They called me Weakheart because between the ages of nine and twelve I developed a growing-child anemia and was excused from gymnasium and active games that might overstrain my heart. Those nicknames were all right, even distinguished. They didn't mean I was queer.

I was teacher's pet up to fourth year, when we had Miss Tin Ear Jenks. We all called her Miss Tin Ear behind her back and laughed because she sometimes marked dumbbells right when they answered wrong and got hopping mad at us for mumbling. Boys in the last row used to mumble any old answer for fun and if the rest of us kept our faces straight they'd get away with it. When there were visitors Miss Tin Ear always called on nice bright girls, like me, who would be sure to answer correctly. Once when the Board of Trustees visited, though, I got rattled and said Augusta was the capital of Georgia.

"Correct," rapped Miss Jenks.

"When I was a boy," one of the trustees remarked, looking at her in an odd way, "Augusta was up in the State of Maine."

Miss Jenks turned purple and glared at me. I think she thought I answered wrong on purpose. She picked on me for the rest of that year. She had carrot-red hair and blue eyes that bugged a little and got bloodshot; it was no fun when she got mad and picked on you. She'd get me so rattled that I'd make mistakes and stutter all over the place, and then she'd pick on me worse than ever.

She gave me poor reports and when she called on me she'd make me stand up and face the class and repeat my answer until I said it distinctly. She scolded me for stuttering and called me a mealy-mouth and a shybird. She said nobody could understand me, that I'd simply have to learn to speak up in this

18

world, that was all. From the way she picked on me you'd think I'd said Augusta was the capital of Georgia just to show up her tin ears in front of the Board of Trustees. But, Judas Priest, that was the kind of thing a boy would do, or a rowdy wild Indian like Pamela Jones, not me. Just imagine me having the nerve to do a thing like that.

I was eleven when my oldest sister was married. I had a lovely pink organdy I called my wedding dress and a long-handled basket of peppermints to pass to guests at the reception.

"What's this about my sweetheart being a weakheart?" Judge Hopkins asked me, helping himself to peppermints. "I understand you're the young lady who faints."

I had never fainted, of course. I had never even felt faint, really — just a sickish little ball of panic in the pit of my stomach sometimes when I wasn't hearing and was afraid someone was going to say, "What's the matter — cotton in your ears?" The dressmaker who made my wedding dress had kept mimbling and mumbling, down on the floor with her mouth full of pins. Several times during fittings I'd pretended to feel faint to explain my not answering her. Feeling faint was a good alibi. Aunt May and Aunt Harriet blamed the excitement of the wedding, combined with my anemia, which I hadn't yet outgrown.

"I'm not your sweetheart," I said to Judge Hopkins.

"By jiminy, something told me I'd been jilted." He scooped up more mints. "You never come in to the Trust Company to see me any more."

That was another thing I pretended — that I didn't love Judge Hopkins as much as I used to and didn't want to go in to see him any more. Because we were wards of the Trust Company, we had to ask him when we wanted extra money for birthdays and holidays and Christmas. Those trips to St. Louis were exciting. We dressed up in our best to see the Judge, and he always hemmed and hawed and teetered judicially in his swivel chair and acted as if we were asking for at least a million dollars. In the end, of course, he gave us whatever we wanted.

Nowadays, however, when I wanted money, I wrote the Judge a letter. I worked hard on my letters, to make them clever and original — my "pretty little letters," he called them. He always sent a check by return mail with a formal reply beginning, "Your pretty little letter of the fourteenth received and contents carefully noted."

The point was that now I was too big to sit on his knee, I couldn't always understand everything the Judge said. I didn't want to risk saying "What?" to him. He might think I wasn't as quick and clever as my sisters. He might think I wasn't the best one in our family, that I was the least one, after all. And I certainly didn't want him to think I couldn't hear. Because I could hear. Not exactly perfectly, but there was nothing to worry about, the new doctor said.

Some people were hard to understand. Judge Hopkins was hard because his thick walrus mustache hid his upper lip and you couldn't see the shape of his words. Also, he talked fast, often with a pipestem between his teeth. I did so wish people would keep things away from their mouths and move their lips and be more animated when they talked. Our town was full of deadpans and mealymouths and shybirds.

Miss Biggs, the town librarian, was a shybird. She was always ducking her head and darting distractedly around the library, her petticoat showing and the placket of her skirt hooked wrong. I couldn't understand a word she said. Mrs. Cahill, who had charge of the Art Museum, was a deadpan. Once I said, "Yes, isn't it?" when Mrs. Cahill directed me to

Gallery A. It was spring and at first I thought she said it was a lovely day. After that I didn't stop at her desk; I found where exhibits were without asking. Mr. Crow at the drugstore was a mealymouth; so was Mr. Siegel, the town photographer, who developed kodak films. I was hardly ever sure what they said, so I'd telephone from home and pretend I'd forgotten when my prescription or my kodak pictures would be ready. I could hear everything everybody said on the telephone — even mealymouths, thank goodness.

I heard better when I could see people's faces; therefore I heard better in the light than in the dark. In firelit rooms or on summer evenings on the porch, I would fall into reverie or pretend to go to sleep. I knew dozens of ways to get people to repeat what they had said without actually asking. For example:

Aunt May: "Will you remember to bring me some wrinkelawreedles on your way home?"

I (dreamily): "From the post office?"

Aunt May (tartly): "Since when does one buy *darning needles* at the post office?"

I tried hard to be as funny as possible all the time. I invented a sidesplitting story to explain why I took Aunt Harriet's crochet pattern to Mrs. Schlee instead of to Mrs. McGee. I was a daydreamer and a woolgatherer; I faked absent-mindedness, boredom, indifference; I faked illness. Fake fainting spells got me out of many a jam. A fake headache or upset stomach made a quick and easy alibi for not hearing. Or I could pretend my head was stuffed up, that I was coming down with a cold. Often that was true. I was still having head colds — far too many for a young lady with my history of scarlet fever and Eustachian-tube inflammation, the new doctor said decisively. He told me to stop having head colds and talked of taking out my tonsils.

It was a precarious life, but I got away with it. Families don't check up much on who hears what. Our family went to church en masse every Sunday, for instance, and of course I never really heard a sermon. But did anybody else?

Besides, the family wanted my hearing to be perfect, just as they wanted my vision to be perfect, my body to be perfect, my front teeth to be perfectly aligned.

Stop slipping your braces off, Aunt May said. If you have crooked teeth, you'll be sorry.

Stop reading all the time and ruining your eyes, Aunt Harriet scolded. If you have to wear glasses, you'll be sorry.

Stop eating so much fudge; your complexion's bumpy, you're much too plump. Don't you want to be slender and beautiful and marry into a fine family like your oldest sister?

Stand up straight. Don't you want to be athletic like your second sister who is so popular and is invited everywhere?

Brush your hair a hundred strokes every night. Don't you want to have thick shiny braids like your sister Ann's?

The aunts knew there was nothing permanently wrong with my complexion, my posture, or my front teeth. They wanted to believe there was nothing permanently wrong with my hearing. They wanted to believe that when they spoke to me and I didn't answer it was because I was a dreamy adolescent who didn't take the trouble to listen.

When I was fourteen, the new doctor took out my tonsils and said there was nothing further to worry about. I'd shot up so fast my ears probably hadn't had a chance to keep up with the rest of me. I'd outgrow my dreaminess and my habit of not listening, just as I'd outgrown my childhood anemia, now vanished without a trace. I'd be all right. Be hearing the grass grow.

Meanwhile I worked steadily at making everyone like me. I

gave away things I'd rather have kept and often swapped hair ribbons and middy ties to my own disadvantage. I helped the girls with their homework and constantly invited them to my house to make fudge. I lent them my books; I had built up a sound collection of thrillers and sentimental trash. I sent away for advertised charm-and-beauty secrets and samples of complexion cream, which I shared freely. I found out all I could about love and marriage from my older sisters and passed the word along.

It was even more important to make boys like me and keep them from guessing my secret. Imagine, I would say to myself with cold shivers — just imagine having a *boy* suspect I didn't hear everything.

One day Roger Evans caught up with me on my way home from school. Roger was one of the best-looking boys at Dean Academy; my best friend Pamela Jones was crazy about him. Roger had taken me to several dances and I felt sure of him, even though I knew Pamela wanted to snag him, but recently I'd seen him walking home with Pamela.

Pamela had changed a lot lately. She had hardly any freckles and her pug nose had turned out all right. She was thinner than I was and much better-looking. Her rowdy voice had grown quieter; often when we spent the night together I had no idea what she was buzzing in my ear about. She was full of secrets. She was always shushing me.

"Judas Priest, pipe down," she'd say. She'd say it at the movies or on the trolley car when the car stopped and I'd go on talking. She'd say it at dances, when the music stopped for intermissions. It made me furious. I didn't talk too loud. Why did she always have to act as if everything were a secret?

Anyhow, I wasn't going to have her snagging Roger Evans. There was an important school dance coming up.

23

I had learned by experience to do all the talking when I walked along the street with a boy. Indoors I could keep voices raised by playing the victrola; outdoors I was in danger of missing what was said. I always walked fast, rattling on at random, trusting to luck that when a boy wanted to ask me to a dance he'd call me on the telephone.

But this time my tongue was tied — transfixed between fear that Roger was going to ask me to the dance (he'd be sure to mumble) and fear that he had already asked Pamela.

He said, "Hello." We scuffed along in silence. My heart jolted against my red sweater and my ears set up such a roaring that I couldn't have heard a fire alarm at ten paces. When we reached my gate, Roger asked me a question. It might have been about algebra. It might have been about football, fudge, or fiddlesticks. It might have been about going to the dance.

I opened my mouth but nothing came of it. What could I say? I certainly wasn't going to say "What?" Well, hardly. And risk the Seven Deadly Words? Risk having a boy — and Roger Evans of all boys — jeer, "What's the matter — cotton in your ears?"

Mentally I ran through my standard dodges — feeling faint, being absent-minded, and so on. They wouldn't do. A big dance was at stake. And I couldn't just stand there.

I swung the gate back and forth. Suddenly I exclaimed, "Wrinkelohwrinkelletdownyourhair!"

"Say, what kind of lingo's that?" Roger demanded.

"Wrinkelingo."

"What's wrinkelingo?"

"Wrinkeli wrinkelthink wrinkelyou wrinkelare wrinkela wrinkelprune," I improvised glibly.

"Come again?"

I repeated it, swinging the gate confidently.

"Wrinkelprune yourself, smarty," he said.

"Yah, wrinkelsap." I swung the gate to and started up the walk.

Roger telephoned that evening and wrinkelasked me to the wrinkeldance. At the dance he and I talked nothing but wrinkelingo. We refined and elaborated it. Ice-cream was wrinkelsauce, punch was wrinkelgrog, a coat a wrinkelwrap, a laugh a wrinkelsnicker. Pamela Jones was Wrinkelpuss. Pamela was furious. Roger hardly danced with her all evening and, when he did, half the time she didn't know what on earth he was talking about.

At my second sister's wedding I wore pink taffeta and carried an old-fashioned bouquet of sweetheart roses.

"How about it?" Judge Hopkins asked, putting an arm around my shoulders. "I'm still waiting for you. Think I've got a chance?"

I shook my head. "Nope. I'm never going to get married."

I was fifteen, and deeply in love with the hero of my favorite sentimental novel — Old Rose and Silver, by Myrtle Reed. My hero was a glamorous young violinist with black eyes and thick shiny black hair. In my daydreams he pursued me through a moonlit rose garden. Like the heroine in the book, I wore a sequin gown to which the moonlight gave a resplendent silver sheen. The violinist wore white tie and tails. As he pursued me, his voice, welling deep from his stiff bosom and trembling with emotion, urged, "Silver Girl! My Silver Girl! Tell me you'll shine for me forever!"

I heard him perfectly, of course. Naturally in my daydreams I always heard perfectly. Who could imagine a heroine of ro-

25

mance, shimmering in a spangled gown, her senses reeling with the fragrance of roses, turning to her pursuing lover and saying "What?"

A heroine of romance could never be hard of hearing. In real life lots of people were, I knew. Wonderful women, like Mrs. George Furness, who bore her affliction bravely. Silly ostriches like Miss Eva Nye and Miss Tin Ear Jenks, who didn't fool anybody but themselves.

Even attractive young married women could be hard of hearing — Caroline Graham, for instance, one of my oldest sister's friends. Caroline had been a Foster, and deafness ran in the Foster family — otosclerosis, it was called. Caroline had been somewhat hard of hearing when she married, and got worse when her first baby came. She made no bones about it; she was always laughing "What?" helplessly, telling how she had to depend on Roy to hear the phone ring and the baby cry. Roy Graham was devoted to her. He'd repeat bids at bridge and tell her the points of jokes she hadn't caught. "You've got to speak up for this gal," he'd say, putting an arm around her. Just the same it was tough on Roy, everybody said — a young broker with contacts to make. It was bound to handicap him socially. His mother had opposed the match for that very reason. Mrs. Graham, Senior, was a widow — a tall, handsome woman; Roy was the image of her. She and my Aunt Harriet were great friends. "Don't tell me, Harriet," I'd heard her wail, "don't tell me my darling boy's going to saddle himself for life, like poor, patient George Furness."

Thank goodness I'd never be like Caroline Graham or Mrs. Furness. Deafness didn't run in our family; I didn't have otosclerosis. I had catarrhal deafness, probably a hangover from scarlet fever, that I would soon outgrow.

The reason I had decided not to marry was that marriage

26

didn't fit in with my plans. Marriage was all right for my sisters, but I wanted something infinitely more thrilling. I was the last one of the family. I still planned to be the best one.

"What are you going to do, if you're never going to get married?" Judge Hopkins asked me.

"I'm going to be the toast of two continents," I told him.

I planned to lure a long queue of suitors down the moon-drenched paths of all the rose gardens of the world. Dressed in cloth of gold, I planned to pause at the royal box at the opera while every head in the vast audience turned to see H.R.H. the Prince of Wales stumble lovestruck to his feet.

In ostrich plumes, I planned to bow right and left as my open carriage swept through the streets of the world's capitals. I planned to be the belle of banquet tables, the reigning beauty at balls, the power behind thrones. I'd need good ears for that.

Although the doctor had said I would outgrow my cotton ears, I myself anticipated something sudden and dramatic, in the nature of a miracle.

I was writing novels myself at this time and in my novels miracles were no surprise to anybody. In one of my novels a hopeless cripple, seeing a child about to perish in a burning building, kicked away his wheel chair and ran, a whole man, to the rescue. In another, a lovely girl, dumb from birth, gained full power of speech in the nick of time to warn her approaching lover, saving him from being fatally crushed by a falling rock.

I was on good terms with God, and it was not unusual in my novels for miracles to be accomplished by prayer. One of my novels was the story of a spoiled rich girl, the meanest little snob in her set, who vowed to become a nun if God would restore her blind father's sight.

That fall I was to go East to boarding school, as my sisters had done, and I wanted perfect hearing before I left. Easterners,

I knew from my sisters' reports, were superior people — suave and socially prominent, scornful of the Middle West and particularly of Missouri, which they pronounced "Mizzudah." Easterners said "eyether" instead of "eether." Easterners thought Middle Westerners were crude. My sisters had disarmed the upstage Easterners, and so could I, I told myself. But I didn't want to have to contend with cotton in my ears.

Easterners were slender and beautiful, like my oldest sister; I was still too plump and my hair still didn't amount to much. Easterners were athletes, like my second sister, with superb muscular co-ordination; I was a dub at all sports. Easterners were clever, like my sister Ann; I was clever, I thought, but what good was cleverness if I couldn't hear the conversation? Easterners lived formally in great, thickly carpeted, dimly lighted houses. They sat murmuring crisp epigrams from the depths of huge chairs placed far apart. Acoustics would be awful in the East, I foresaw. I might as well try to hear the grass grow.

I made a bargain with God. I told Him that if He would give me perfect hearing by the following October 12th, the day my Eastern school opened, I would devote my entire life to Him. Being a Protestant, I didn't offer to become a nun. I did, however, mention going as a missionary to China.

I didn't want to go as a missionary to China. I wanted to shop for sequins, cloth of gold, black satin, and plumes. But I needed perfect hearing by October 12th. If worst came to worst I could go to China. I saw myself dressed in white, borne by coolies to the royal palace to convert the Emperor to Christianity. Compared to my other plans it seemed dreary.

Time enough to decide, however, I told myself, when I had had my miracle. When I had had my miracle and could hear perfectly like everybody else maybe I could just skip China.

3

"HEY! Forget to wash those ears last Saturday?"
This was Stella, my boarding-school roommate. Stella
was an Easterner; she came from New Haven. But she wasn't
at all upstage. She was small and blond, pretty as an angel, hearty
as a sailor. She had four brothers, two at Yale and two in prep
school, from whom she had learned to smoke and to say "sonofabitch."

Her brothers had also molded Stella's sense of humor. Her
favorite jokes involved calling all teachers picklepusses, vowing
her roommate snored, insisting that Saturday night was bath
night. She had a clear voice that I heard easily, but, if by chance
she said something and I didn't answer, she never thought twice
about it. She had livelier concerns than the state of my hearing.
She'd sing out, "Hey, what's today — Friday? Almost time to
wash those ears."

I didn't mind being teased about snoring, because I snored

purposely. Stella was a great whisperer after lights out and sleep was my alibi for not answering. It occurred to me, too, that she might be right about my washing my ears. Maybe I hadn't been washing them hard enough. I began scrubbing them night and morning, seven times in one direction, seven in the other; it seemed to me my hearing sharpened.

Drake School was in Connecticut, an hour's train ride from New York City. It was run by two sisters, Miss Drake and Miss Eunice Drake. Both women were very tall and slender, with beautiful piled-up white hair. They were erect and authoritative — as formidable as my Aunt Harriet and more so — exactly what I had expected Easterners to be. Miss Drake directed the school and Miss Eunice taught Reading and Speaking; she had studied for the stage.

Miss Eunice ignored me and I took that as my lot. Why shouldn't she ignore me? Wasn't I much too plump? Wasn't my hair too soft and fine to amount to anything? Didn't I come from the Middle West?

I was surprised when Stella told me Miss Eunice didn't hear well; I hadn't realized it. I was so sure Easterners were superior people that it hadn't occurred to me an Easterner would be hard of hearing. It seemed Miss Eunice had been somewhat deafened by illness at the outset of a promising career as a Shakespearean actress. You weren't supposed to let on you knew it, Stella said.

One day in Reading and Speaking class Miss Eunice asked me to read Milton's sonnet on his blindness. Before I rattled half through the familiar "When I consider how my light is spent," she stopped me.

She gazed around the class. Her eyes were magnificent — large and dark and intensely alive. Her voice was velvet and honey and violincellos.

30

"Is theyah anyone," she demanded, "who undahstahnds what eyetha Mr. Milton or this young lady from Mizzudah is talking about?"

My voice was babyish and immatuah, she said. Veddy sweet for a child of five, but I was fifteen, was I not? She ridiculed my Midwestern accent. Slim and erect, breathing smoothly from her own consummately controlled diaphragm, she ridiculed my posture, my breathing, my figure, and everything about me.

It was bliss. Shivering happily while the goddess destroyed my ego, I mentally re-created myself in her divine image. I vowed to use broad a's, deepen my breathing, shed every vestige of Missouri twang. I vowed to lose ten pounds, brush my hair a hundred strokes daily, walk around the room fifteen minutes every night with a book on my head, and become a great Shakespearean actress.

Stella would giggle, watching me step gingerly around in pink-and-white striped pajamas, my well-brushed hair in kid curlers, *Webster's Collegiate Dictionary* balanced on my head. Stella herself would be sprawled on her bed gorging chocolate cookies swiped from the school pantry. She, of course, was no more impressed by Miss Eunice than she was by any other pickle-puss.

On Saturday evenings Miss Eunice regularly gave Shakespeare readings in the great hall. Often as we sat on the floor at her feet waiting for the reading to begin, Stella would while away the time by reciting her own special version of the *Hamlet* soliloquy. She had picked it up from her brothers, and it went:

"To be a sonofabitch or not to be a sonofabitch
That is a sonofabitch of a question."

She would recite the entire soliloquy, liberally sprinkling

31

sonofabitches, with demure hands folded in her lap, an innocent expression on her pure sweet angel face. The effect was sidesplitting because, of course, Miss Eunice would be sitting there looking right at Stella, but oblivious, not hearing a word she said.

Naturally Stella never did the soliloquy when there was any other picklepuss within earshot; she'd probably have been expelled from school for saying "sonofabitch." She'd certainly have been expelled for making fun of Miss Eunice's deafness; we weren't supposed to be aware of it and the rest of us pretended not to be.

Sitting at Miss Eunice's feet on Saturday evenings and really hearing Shakespeare for the first time was so exciting it made my spine tingle. I could hardly believe this was the same Shakespeare I had been used to all my life. Miss Eunice read *Hamlet* and *The Merchant of Venice* and *Macbeth* — all of which I'd seen half a dozen times; our family went en masse to Shakespeare when Sothern and Marlowe or Robert Mantell were in St. Louis. To me, Shakespeare was something inaudible to sit through like church — so boring that I usually had the exact center of the ceiling estimated and an imaginary staple driven in for the imaginary rope ladder of my old friend, the gone-but-not-forgotten Wrinkel, by the middle of Act One.

Listening to Miss Eunice, I sat up straight. I was Ophelia, Portia, Lady Macbeth. I was tall and slender with magnificent, alive dark eyes and a voice like velvet and honey and violincellos. My audience went wild; applause was riotous. Ushers staggered under their floral loads. Men in white ties paced my dressing room; outside, students unhorsed my carriage to draw me home. I cared little for that. My eyes were for my beloved coach, Miss Eunice Drake, who stood proudly in the wings. I ran to her.

"It was not I, but you," I cried.

"God bless you, child." She smiled serenely. "You have redeemed my failure."

That was an agreeable daydream on two counts. I was in love with John Barrymore. As a great Shakespearean actress I would be in a position not only to redeem Miss Eunice's failure but, someday, to be Ophelia to John's Hamlet, and Mrs. Barrymore if I liked. My love for John dated from an exceptionally golden Saturday afternoon when Stella's father took six of us to lunch at the Waldorf-Astoria and to see Barrymore play du Maurier's *Peter Ibbetson.*

Stella's father apologized for our seats; they were in the front row of the orchestra — all he had been able to get. He hoped it wouldn't spoil the play for us to be so close to all the grease paint. I had never sat in the first row. For the first time in my life I could relax in the theatre and really know what a play was about. I was not soon again to be so fortunate. We went often to the theatre from Drake School, both chaperoned and unchaperoned, but we sat well behind the tenth row and all too frequently in the balcony.

We were taken in groups to concerts, to the opera, to Mary Pickford and William S. Hart movies, and to improving plays. Movies, being silent, were fine. Concerts were all right; nobody could check up on how clearly I heard Beethoven. Opera was no trouble because it was in Italian or French, which I didn't have to pretend to understand. If the play was by someone already published like Barrie or Shaw, I could read it beforehand.

But Stella hungered for unapproved musical shows and sophis-ticated drawing-room comedies, and she had an aunt in New York — glamorous Gretta Hammond, a well-known concert pianist — who was willing to be our technical chaperon so long as we never went near her. Stella and I went to the theatre so often that our allowances couldn't encompass orchestra seats;

33

besides, some picklepuss from school might see us unchaperoned and report us. So many a Saturday afternoon found us chewing caramels aloft in some unapproved balcony while Stella reveled in off-color jokes and marital triangles and I laughed heartily whenever she did.

Musical shows were all right; there was plenty to see and the plot didn't matter. Plays dragged; I'd get bored imagining, and itch to know what the play was about. Naturally I never asked. During intermissions I might inquire offhand what Stella thought would happen next; with luck I'd get an inkling of what had already happened. That is, if I heard what Stella said.

I did so wish people wouldn't talk in subdued tones during intermissions. The curtain fell. Applause. Sudden hush. Then animated talk — but low-pitched, as if the strangers in neighboring seats might be enemy spies. This was true not just between acts at the theatre. Life was full of intermissions.

At football games your companions' voices were comfortably audible above the yelling, singing, and cheering. At dances you could hear everything your partners said as long as the orchestra played. Then came the intermission, the sudden lull. Voices dropped automatically.

I had danger zones mentally charted under various headings. One such heading was:

INTERMISSIONS, HOW TO COPE WITH

1. Theatre, concert, opera, etc.
   a. Concentrate on absorbed reading of program or libretto
   b. Sit spellbound, implying reluctance to come back to earth
   c. Rearrange wraps; hunt for something on the floor
   d. Keep companion lockjawed and silent with large pieces of chewy candy.

34

e. Pretend to be amusedly eavesdropping on the conversation at your other side
f. Visit ladies' room and water-cooler
g. Spin monologue on
   (1) Plays, concerts, operas previously attended
   (2) Funny-looking people in the audience
   (3) Adventures (real or imaginary) encountered on trip to and from ladies' room

2. Football Games
   a. Be chilly. Muffle ears comically in scarf or laprobe
   b. Have foot go to sleep. Create noise and laughter by stamping
   c. Divert escort's attention to getting and consuming of coffee, hot dogs, etc.
   d. Do tricks with matches or handkerchiefs. Encourage escort to do tricks. Tear up program; make and sail paper darts

3. Dances
   a. Continue to sing tune last played
   b. Ask to be shown a new dance step
   c. Play cagey; pretend you won't answer questions; you know the answer but you're not telling
   d. Read your partner's palm
   e. Powder your nose; lose something; remember you have to telephone; how about some punch?

Even in the East, I told myself with satisfaction, my secret remained a secret. Nobody, I felt sure, had the least idea that I was partially deaf, though some of the girls had the idea that I was part Indian.

Few of them had traveled west of the Adirondacks. They thought Missouri was full of Indians, and I told them this was

35

so. When I didn't hear what somebody said, I assumed a glum Indian expression and made a noncommittal Indian reply such as "Ugh!" or "How!" This was so well liked that I invented an Uncle Spencer who had married an Indian princess named Menowannaplay. My Uncle Spencer stories, done in Indian dialect, were so popular that I was cast as an Indian medicine man in the school pageant. The medicine man had only one line and I didn't get to say it, as it turned out. When the time came I was so excited I missed my cue; I simply didn't hear it. Everybody laughed at me for getting stage fright.

School had its pitfalls, among them my old enemy athletics. Sports were required. I was no good at hockey, baseball, or tennis. Fear of betraying that I hadn't heard the score and wasn't sure of shouts and signals kept me tense and clumsy. Like any number of people with poor hearing, I had a poor sense of balance; horseback riding and bicycling scared the wits out of me. I solved the problem by going out for golf. I was a dub, and we carried our own clubs, so I could play alone. In winter I took refuge inside a sound-proof rubber cap and splashed in the swimming pool.

Meals were another pitfall, particularly dinner. We dined at large tables, and voices were ladylike. Between courses came lulls like theatre intermissions. I worked out safety techniques:

DINNER LULLS, HOW TO COPE WITH

a. Sit next to a Head with a good, sharp voice, like Picklepuss Reeves
b. Choke, cough, or get hiccups, if someone asks you a direct question
c. Take hold of the conversation yourself. Ask someone to tell a story you have already heard. Ask questions the answers to which you already know

36

I was a favorite with the sharp-voiced English teacher, Pickle-puss Reeves. She had lived in China, and she often invited me to her room to drink jasmine tea from cups without handles. She was the daughter of missionaries. The more I learned about missionary life the drearier it sounded, but I was keeping an open mind on that score. I was still on good terms with God.

There had been a delay on my miracle. So far I was getting along all right. I could hold out until time to go to college, I told myself, but no longer. I was going to a large New England college and I'd need perfect hearing in New England. Boston intellectuals would speak low.

I had confidence in God and I was careful not to antagonize Him. I behaved myself. No sense in taking chances with my miracle. Besides, sin involved the two pitfalls I was most chary of — whispering and darkness.

Petting was out. So was smoking, which Stella and the others did after lights out with surreptitious whispers on the roof outside the bathroom window. I did swipe my share of chocolate cookies from the school pantry. Determined to lose ten pounds for Miss Eunice Drake's sake, I ate delicately at meals and was ravenous by midnight. Nor was I above a guilty midnight ride when one of Stella's prep-school brothers or friends of brothers managed to swipe his family's car. On such a ride a boy could even put his arm around me. But stop the car? Stop the hum of the motor above which voices were easily audible? Not with me along.

If the car did stop, I knew a fancy tenor to "Moonlight Bay." Harmony singing was the solution to many a dangerous lull, especially during holiday and summer vacations when I visited classmates in the country or at the shore. To my safety techniques I added an important category headed HARMONY SINGING, PLACES TO RELY ON, under which I listed parked cars, firelit

37

rooms, porch swings, beaches, canoes and rowboats, moonlight picnics, and the like.

I had some narrow escapes, but on the whole the two years at Drake School went off smoothly. Easterners thought I was amusing, suprising, moody, sometimes daffy, sometimes difficult, sometimes dense; but nobody thought I didn't hear well. At least I didn't think they did.

I met people at the wrong place or showed up on the wrong train occasionally, but in the East as well as at home I had built up a reputation for absent-mindedness. I once heard "week-end guest" as "quite a mess" and got into quite a mess myself as a result.

As always, I worked hard at being nice. I let myself in for some dull chores that way. One spring I let myself in for an endless series of botany walks, carrying a tin box, collecting specimens of *Dryopteris filix-mas* (Boston fern) and maidenhair (*Adiantum pedatum*). I loathed ferns and mud and dead leaves, but I had to go. Some soft-spoken picklepuss had asked me to do something or other and I said Yes, just to be nice. When I found out what I'd agreed to do, I kicked myself, but there was nothing for it but to follow through. I wasn't going to let on I'd answered without hearing the question, was I?

Moreover, I got even with botany. Slogging through mud and digging reluctantly in slippery leaf mold for *Dryopteris filix-mas*, I grimly planned a theme for English class. I planned it in the elegant, high-pitched manner of Max Beerbohm, whom I'd discovered recently and adopted as my literary idol. The theme was a success — a mock-serious tirade against ferns, mud, dead leaves, moss, Latin names, and everything that had to do with botany walks. I called it "Oh, Dryopteris!" Picklepuss Reeves gave me A on it and it was published in the *Drake School Annual*.

You could work off grudges in writing, I discovered. You could say whatever you pleased in writing, as long as you kept it funny and exaggerated. I followed "Oh, Dryopteris!" with a tirade against my enemy athletics. It was silly, I said, for people to dash around after balls; it made them all red in the face. I denounced theatre intermissions, affirming that they encouraged excess lemonade drinking. I needled my archenemies, librarians and employees of art museums, not because they were shybirds and deadpans (Heaven forbid that I should hint at such matters) but because they wore tacky clothes. Picklepuss Reeves was pleased. She said I should develop this mock-serious vein — I might have the making of a humorous writer.

I more than redeemed my stage fright as Indian medicine man in the third-year pageant by my success in the Commencement Play.

I had never been straighter or more slender. For months I'd been walking fifteen minutes a day with a book on my head. Two weeks before the play those of us who were to wear men's costumes went on a spartan diet. We also had fencing lessons, which helped coax our weight down; the play was Booth Tarkington's *Monsieur Beaucaire*, which involved skirmishing with swords.

Fortified by pale-blue satin breeches, my own unsatisfactory hair concealed under a lovely curled white powdered wig, I felt self-confident, every inch an actress. I moved with the sure ease and polished grace of the French courtier I was supposed to represent. I spoke my lines ringingly, breathing from the diaphragm, using broad a's, hoping against passionate hope that at long last Miss Eunice Drake would notice me.

39

Wounded in Act Three by the sword-thrust of my rival, I groaned my final exit line (It was "Curse you, hound — the devil fought with you!") with accent, voice-production, and tone which held no faintest tincture of Missouri.

I glanced at Miss Eunice, who stood proudly in the wings. She had coached our play, of course. Her magnificent dark eyes shone. She smiled serenely. It was the moment, in my favorite daydream, when I ran to her and she said, "Bless you, my child," However, as usual, Miss Eunice ignored me.

She had ignored me completely, ever since my first class recitation when I botched "When I consider how my light is spent." She gave me no further criticism, ever, except a sigh when I finished reading and a disreputable D in her course. She didn't like me. I knew why. It was the Nyes, back home, and Mrs. Furness, and Miss Tin Ear Jenks all over again. It was because I didn't speak up — because I was a shybird and a mealymouth.

The girls Miss Eunice liked were the ones with natural poise and animation and clear, well-placed voices. Girls like Stella, though what Miss Eunice would have thought of Stella if she'd known about the Hamlet soliloquy . . .

"Hey, you know what?" Stella said, when Commencement was over and we were packing our trunks to leave school. "I almost didn't graduate. Picklepuss Eunice nearly flunked me out."

"What do you mean?" I asked. Stella's marks were much better than mine were.

"She gave me a veddy serious talking to. Said she had gravely considahed withholding my diploma. Because of my unladylike sense of humah. And my outrageous language."

"Don't tell me she ever heard 'To be or not to be.' "

Stella nodded.

40

"You mean to say she sat there and heard it and never let on?"

"Oh, she wouldn't have deigned. She was veddy, veddy contemptuous."

"But, Stella" — I was flabbergasted — "how could she have heard it?"

Stella shrugged. "Maybe she washes her ears on Saturday."

I couldn't figure it out. Was Miss Eunice not really hard of hearing? Was she hard of hearing only some of the time? Was she play-acting?

"Well, to be a sonofabitch!" I marveled.

Stella giggled. "Or not to be a sonofabitch."

It was a sonofabitch of a question. Because neither Stella nor I, of course, had any idea there was such a thing as understanding what people said by watching their mouths. We had never heard of lip reading.

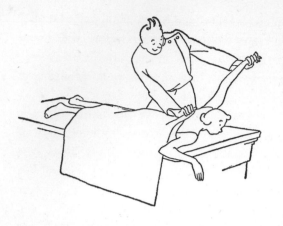

4

I WOULD have learned more in college if I'd had a name beginning with A or B and thus come naturally by a front-row seat in classes. Most of my classes were large. Seating was alphabetical. Sitting far back among the W's, I passed many a lecture hour doodling around the edges of a clean notebook page, examining the ceiling to find its exact center and thinking what magnificent gibberish my old friend Wrinkel would have made of lectures on Chaucer and Michelangelo and Plato's Theory of the Absolute Good.

After class I read up on Chaucer and Michelangelo and Plato in the library. To make sure what lectures were about, I borrowed my neighbors' notes. My immediate concern at the beginning of any course was to be awfully nice to the W's on either side of me and throw myself on their good nature as a likable scatterbrain who couldn't take decent notes.

It was just as well I was a W, I told myself at the beginning of

Freshman year. I certainly didn't want anyone in college to get the idea I had cotton ears, and my presence in the back row of classes was constant proof that I could hear all right. Students who couldn't hear well, like Marge Martin, were given special seats in the center of the front row.

Marge Martin gave me the willies. She was very pale, with blond hair and staring pale-blue eyes. She reminded me a little of Alice Hart, the girl who had been electrocuted years ago, back home. Marge talked in a flat voice that was sometimes so faint no one could hear it and sometimes so shrill that people turned to look at her. That was because she couldn't hear herself accurately, people said, and therefore couldn't regulate her voice.

She had been deafened in childhood; her head had been injured in a coasting accident and the auditory nerve had been damaged. She had studied lip reading and could understand what people said by watching their mouths and the expressions on their faces. It was wonderful, everybody said, to think of her having courage to tackle college with such a handicap. Everybody went out of the way to be nice to her. She was wonderful, everybody said.

Whenever I met wonderful Marge Martin on campus I smiled and sang out, "Hello, how are you?" heartily and hurried past. I didn't want to stop and talk to her if I could help it. It was embarrassing. You didn't know whether to shout or mouth words silently, and it gave you a funny feeling to have her watching your lips.

Besides, I didn't want to associate even casually with Marge. Somebody like nauseous Victorine Parry might get the idea we were alike, that our voices sounded alike, or something. I boiled with hatred every time I thought of nauseous Victorine Parry, who had sat next to me during College Board examinations the

43

summer before. Victorine may have been a lovely girl. Undoubtedly her parents, presumably at least a few friends, cherished Victorine. I, myself, wished her dead. She was a long spindle-legged girl with an unwholesome complexion. She had fuzzy yellow hair puffed way out over her ears. But I didn't wish her dead for those reasons. I wished her dead because on a hot summer day in a drugstore in Chicago she knocked the bottom out of my world.

I happened to take my College Board exams in Chicago, where I knew no one. Since we sat side by side, Victorine and I went to the corner drugstore to lunch together the first day, between English and Chemistry. Her lunch was a cup of hot milk. She felt too nauseous for words, she told me. She had a tipped pelvis and her insides were on a slant.

Next day, between French and Mathematics, Victorine had corned beef on rye bread with mustard and coleslaw and a strawberry ice-cream soda. She had been to Dr. Fletcher, her chiropractor, she announced, and felt fine.

"Why don't you try a chiropractor?" she asked me, chewing corned beef, giving no slightest indication that she was about to knock the bottom out of my world. "Dr. Fletcher told me he's curing one of his patients of deafness."

My heart skittered, in panic, against my ribs. What did she mean?

"My dad's deaf," she revealed. "I can spot a deaf person anywhere. That soft voice of yours. And that trick of letting your sentences trail off — not finishing them. Dad does that all the time."

The bottom fell out of my world. What was she saying? That she'd spotted me for a deaf person? That it was perfectly plain to anyone that I didn't hear well? That wasn't so. It couldn't be so. Nobody could possibly guess I didn't hear well; I had every-

44

body bluffed. Besides, I could hear all right. Nobody could call me a deaf person. Nobody with long spindle legs and a bad complexion and fuzzy yellow hair that looked as if she never brushed it.

My head spun with fury. Did I trail my sentences? I did, often. Often I'd see, from the expression on another person's face, that I was talking on the wrong track, that I'd misheard something. When that happened, if I trailed my words vaguely, nine times out of ten the other person would finish the sentence, putting me on the right track again. Heaven knows I knew my voice was too soft. I tried to talk louder, but I was afraid of talking too loud and being shushed, the way Pamela Jones used to shush me when we were kids.

"Dad's wonderful," Victorine was saying. "He can't hear thunder without an earphone and not very much even with an earphone, but he keeps trying. He's got our dining-room table and his favorite chair in the living-room all wired up for sound; you can't move without tripping over electric wires and storage batteries. Just lately one of the hearing-aid companies came out with a portable model that he can carry around in a black box. It weighs seven pounds and has a big black receiver on a headband. Dad looks like a walking telephone operator in it."

She went on chewing and talking. "Hearing aids aren't much good yet — they're still in their infancy, Dad says. Dad once met Alexander Graham Bell. Did you know Bell invented the telephone by accident when he was trying to invent an earphone for his wife? Mrs. Bell was a wonderful woman — very deaf."

"Really? We'd better be getting back for the Math exam," I said freezingly.

In the examination room I chose a different seat, turned my back on Victorine, and wished her dead. She was a pig, I told myself. She could go to blazes. She could go straight to Mrs.

45

Alexander Graham Bell. I'd never seen her before. I'd never see her again. She was nauseous. If she kept gorging corned-beef sandwiches like such a pig, maybe she'd choke to death.

I must be more careful, that was all. I must make myself talk louder. Now that I knew trailing sentences were a giveaway, I must stop letting mine trail. And I must find a chiropractor.

I went to Boston to look for one as soon as I was settled in college. It gave me a delicious sense of sin. Aunt May and Aunt Harriet were suspicious of chiropractors — as they were suspicious of cafeterias, revival meetings, and labor unions — because they seemed to attract so many poor people. Even after I was cured, I realized, I could never let the aunts find out I'd been to a chiropractor.

Dr. Dexter was a buoyant young Boston chiropractor with an upstanding pompadour, immaculate white shoes, and a starched white jacket, cut Russian-blouse style, with a high neck. He looked as if he had stepped from the chorus of the *Chauve Souris*.

"You're not deaf," he caroled exuberantly. "A pretty girl like you? That's ridiculous. How old are you — eighteen? Deafness is for old ladies — 'Hey? What say?' " He cupped a hand comically behind one ear, taking off a deaf old lady.

"Of course I'm not deaf." I laughed. "It's just that I get a lot of head colds and feel as if my ears were stuffed with cotton."

"We'll fix you up." He nodded. He unrolled a colored chart of the human body showing nerves radiating out from the spinal column and explained how chiropractic adjustment of the vertebrae set the spinal cord humming and put the whole body in tune. He didn't examine my ears. Didn't know a thing about ears, he said. Didn't want to. "You come in here once a

46

week," he said. "We'll get your spinal cord humming. Your ears'll take care of themselves."

Naturally I didn't tell my friends I was going to Dr. Dexter to have my hearing fixed up. I told them I had a tipped pelvis and often felt too nauseated for words. Fake nausea was a good alibi for not hearing in chapel and in the college auditorium. Occasionally, too, it was useful when I was called on in class.

Sometimes, in my classes, there would be silence. The instructor's eyes on me questioningly. A room full of inquiring heads turning to stare. Judas Priest, I'd been called on. I'd been called on and I had no ghost of an idea what the question was.

When this happened, I might give a start, indicating that I'd been caught woolgathering. The question would be repeated and I might hear it the second time. Better still, the instructor might turn impatiently to someone else. Or I might fake nausea — passing a hand over my forehead and murmuring I was sorry, I felt a little ill. This would not be entirely untrue. At such moments I would feel the same sickish little ball of panic in the pit of my stomach that I'd felt when I was eleven and the dressmaker who was fitting my pink organdy wedding dress kept mimbling and mumbling, down on the floor with her mouth full of pins.

Thank goodness, such moments were rare. I did everything humanly possible all through college to avoid recitation. I took as many straight lecture courses as the curriculum allowed, regardless of whether the subject interested me. I took all the pipe courses given by professors who were known not to care how often you cut class or whether you recited or not. In courses that involved recitation I used every dodge I could think of to avoid being called on — everything from sliding way down in my seat to stopping at the instructor's desk before class to explain hoarsely that I had a bad cold (I had a lot of them in spite

47

of my weekly visits to Dr. Dexter) and couldn't speak above a whisper.

By Sophomore year I'd lost faith in chiropractic. Dr. Dexter was as buoyant as ever. He had my spinal cord humming, but my ears weren't taking care of themselves. I inquired offhand at the college infirmary for the name of the best ear specialist in Boston and began regular appointments with him. I told my friends I had anemia. That gave me carte blanche to fake a few useful fainting spells. If I hadn't been able to fake a fainting spell Junior year when I was initiated into a secret society, I don't know what I'd have done; the initiation went on in whispers in a room pitch-black except for a tiny ceremonial lamp. Later I invented a low-grade fever to cover all pseudo-indisposition and explain why I was taking so much quinine.

I had read in Dr. Bingle's syndicated newspaper health column that quinine was a cure for impaired hearing, so I tried it. I got a bad scare; I had no hearing at all for several hours. I never took quinine again, but I kept on saying I did. It made a good alibi because nearly everyone had taken quinine at some time and knew it made you temporarily deaf. I used the quinine alibi off and on for years. In fact, it wasn't until much later when I lived among New York sophisticates and learned that it is a drug frequently associated with abortions that I finally gave quinine up.

Sophomore year I was again planning to marry my doctor. This was Boston's great otologist, Dr. Richardson, who had studied in Vienna with the world-famous Dr. Abraham Leopold.

"What's this — measles, diphtheria?" Dr. Richardson asked, the first time I went to see him. He slanted the round mirror on his forehead so he could see inside my ears. He had deep-set gray eyes and thick snow-white hair and eyebrows. He had a

48

lovely deep voice and made me feel poised and important because he didn't talk down to me. "Scarlet fever, probably. That's
the villain. Causes more ear trouble than any other childhood
disease."

He rumbled, "I wish Leopold in Vienna could have a go at
you. We don't know much about progressive deafness, you know.
But Leopold's doing wonders with some of these catarrhal cases."

He made me say, "Kay, kay, kay," while he inflated my Eustachian tubes with air from a rubber bulb. Before and after
this treatment he tested my hearing with tuning forks of different sizes.

"Seems better," he said. "Come in once a week. If inflation
helps, I may try a vibration treatment of Leopold's."

"How long will it take?" I asked.

"Oh — no time at all. Ten or fifteen minutes."

"I mean how long will it take to get my hearing up to
normal?"

"Looking for a miracle, are you?"

I nodded emphatically.

"Most of my patients are," he said. "Funny about the hard of
hearing. Because their impairment isn't visible they think it
isn't real. They think at most it's only temporary — that the
next doctor or the next drug they try will surely cure them."

He shoved the round mirror back from his forehead.

"The hard of hearing are the most stubborn and the most
gullible people in the world. They'll try anything — even sane,
otherwise intelligent, sensible people who ought to have gump-
tion enough to know better. They'll try anything from first-rate
otologists to high-priced charlatans to hocus-pocus and mail-
order quackery. They believe in miracles. They never seem to
stop believing in miracles until they go broke or die."

"Miracles happen," I assured him, suddenly recalling the

49

woman in Aunt Harriet's newspaper story who had her scissors struck by lightning.

"Sometimes," he agreed. "I had one just the other day. A young married woman. Believe it or not, cotton had been accidentally left in her ears sometime during childhood and was still in there, embedded in wax. Naturally she couldn't hear well. When I washed out the wax and she suddenly heard the elevators running in the hall outside, she was so happy she began to cry. So did her husband. They thought they'd had a miracle, all right." He smiled at me. "I wish there were more miracles."

"You said Dr. Leopold did wonders," I reminded him.

"He seems to, with some of his cases. May be partly psychological — I don't know. They're flocking to him in droves. Well — come in once a week. We'll do what we can. Keep you from getting any worse, anyhow. After you've finished college — who knows? Maybe we'll ship you across to Vienna."

I decided to marry Dr. Richardson. In a sense I would be sacrificing myself, because he was so much older than I was. But what a pleasure to be married to a man who knew such a lot and had such a lovely voice. I had been going to a series of dances with Harvard undergraduates. All they thought about was football and hip flasks and they mumbled so I wanted to murder them.

Dr. Richardson was well past sixty. During my treatments I would watch him fondly, thinking how faithfully I would minister to him during the closing years of his life. The Leopold treatment hurt like the dickens, but I didn't mind; in imagination I repaid pain with gentleness.

After his death, I would of course remarry. With perfect hearing, I could marry — oh, the Prince of Wales. If by any chance my hearing had not been completely restored by Dr. Richardson, I'd go to Vienna and put myself into the hands of Dr.

Abraham Leopold. While I was about it, I might as well put myself into the hands, also, of the Viennese gland specialist who, according to recent reports, had discovered the secret of eternal youth.

Dr. Richardson liked me because I could take so much punishment. He always called me his prize patient. At one point a test seemed to indicate some improvement in my hearing. He was so pleased he clapped me on the shoulder and exclaimed, "Good girl! Maybe you won't be a deaf old lady after all."

The clap on my shoulder surprised me in the middle of gland treatments in daydream Vienna.

"Goodness gracious, I'm never going to be old," I said, adding in a burst of sudden unholy glee, — "and I'll tell you something else I'm never going to be. I'm never going to be wonderful."

I was so sick of the word wonderful. Wonderful Marge Martin. You kept hearing how wonderful she was. She'd been elected vice-president of our class. She'd been appointed to Student Council — a great honor. A reporter from a Boston newspaper had interviewed her for one of a series of articles on unusual college students. After college Marge was going to do social service work among the deafened, she told the reporter. Helping others like herself was her interest in life. How wonderful, said everyone, including, of all people, my good friend Anna Mary Dodge — Anna Mary, whose own interests in life were the Dartmouth Winter Carnival, tea dancing at the Copley Plaza in Boston, and getting herself invited to the horsy house party one of our classmates, Belle Cunningham, was giving during Hunt Week at her family's place in Maryland.

Wonderful, my eye. If I had to be hard of hearing (which I didn't, thanks to Dr. Richardson and, if necessary, Dr. Leopold) I'd never be wonderful about it, I told myself. I'd simply skip it.

51

I'd go to live in Paris. A hard-of-hearing person would be perfectly safe living in Paris. The French were lighthearted; they would shrug off one's mistakes, laugh aside one's blunders. I'd spend my days at sidewalk cafés and my evenings in gay, glittering gold-and-crystal restaurants. I'd flirt with a boulevardier, dance with a gigolo.

I'd marry a Frenchman — a man of the world, debonair and polished, a connoisseur of food and wine. We'd have a smart town house in the Etoile section of Paris, a château in Brittany, and a villa on the Riviera. I'd be vivacious and charming — gowns by Molyneux, hats by Patou. No one — not even my husband — would suspect I had cotton in my ears. Why should they? I'd be a foreigner. When I didn't hear, when I looked puzzled and said "Pardon?" they'd assume, as my French professor at college, Madame Dupont, assumed, that I was one of those Americans who had no ear for French.

Madame Dupont was my great friend. We lived in the same college dormitory and I sat at her table in the dining room. She was tiny and animated, adorably chic and dashing, and whether she spoke French or English she always talked quite loudly, as one instinctively does among foreigners.

French was one of my favorite subjects. I could read it fluently and I did some acceptable translations of French poetry. Madame Dupont was baffled by my slowness with spoken French. I had the heart for French, she declared. I had the spirit. It must be that I did not have the ear.

She urged me to go to Paris the summer following my Junior year to try to improve my spoken French. She could recommend a pension "très, très, TRÈS comme il faut," not two blocks from the Sorbonne. But Aunt May and Aunt Harriet wouldn't hear of Paris. They'd worry themselves sick, they said. Instead, they planned a tour of the West for that summer and worried themselves sick because on the train between Denver and San Francisco I spent all my time on the observation platform with an ex-serviceman from Texas named Jim Fisher.

Jim was nothing like the tall, handsome, black-haired young violinist in Myrtle Reed's *Old Rose and Silver* who pursued me through the moon-drenched rose gardens of my sixteen-year-old daydreams and called me Silver Girl. Jim was stocky, average height, average good-looking, with a small mustache and the beginning of early baldness. He pursued me through the San Francisco Limited to the observation platform and called me Honey.

He said "Yes, ma'am" and "No, ma'am" to Aunt Harriet and Aunt May. They didn't awe him, though; he'd been through Belleau Wood and Château-Thierry. When the aunts looked haughty and summoned me in from the observation platform, Jim would smile a warm Texas smile and say in his Texas drawl, "Restez-vous, folks, restez-vous. Theah is no dangah." That was his favorite expression. He'd picked it up from a Negro fire-eater at a café in Paris after the Armistice. It made the aunts furious.

The observation platform might have been made to my order. Hour after hour the train rushed on without stopping, its fine free racket keeping Jim's drawling voice right up where I could hear it. Even my archenemy darkness was licked on the observation platform, since the train, as if for my special benefit, rushed as noisily by night as it did by day.

Jim and I told our secrets. I admitted that I was planning to be a really good writer — that as a first step I had ideas for a series of humorous essays I hoped to publish in the *Atlantic Monthly*. Jim admitted that his degree in engineering was his first step toward tearing apart the present world and building a really good one.

53

We confessed weaknesses, brought our painful flaws to light. Jim said he was mighty touchy about getting bald. I scoffed at him. Baldness was nothing, I said. We held hands. The last evening Jim kissed me. The aunts were so upset that the minute we reached San Francisco they whisked me off to Portland, Oregon.

"Write to me," I said to Jim, and soon his first letter came — a grand letter, tender and sprightly. Jim had a real gift for words. His letters followed me throughout the Western trip and East to college in September. He wrote me two letters a week and a special delivery every Sunday. I answered every letter the day it came.

My favorite book just then was George Moore's *Héloïse and Abélard* — that calm, serene, and infinitely poignant story of two lovers destined to spend their lives apart. Jim continued to call me Honey, but as time went on I felt a lot like Héloïse. I took it for granted that I'd never see Jim again. I didn't want to see him. I wanted to get three well-written love letters every week and send three well-written love letters in return.

I was feeling every inch a writer and was working on my series of essays in the high-pitched, mock-serious manner that Pickleface Reeves at Drake School had liked. The first was a tirade against an enemy I found particularly horrid in New England: winter sports. My friends were always at me vigorously to go skiing; I tried it and fell on my head. Those were years when everything Russian was popular; I called my essay "Ski? Whyski?" and proposed a world revolution against the great outdoors. An *Atlantic Monthly* editor liked the piece and asked me to send him more.

If eventually I became a really good writer, I told myself, my correspondence with Jim Fisher might be unearthed and published. It might make a vignette of the early 1920's. I hoped Jim would soon ask me to marry him; it would liven the letters if we were engaged. There would be no danger of my ever marrying him. "Restez-vous, folks, restez-vous," I mentally reassured Aunt May and Aunt Harriet. Imagine marrying an unglamorous engineer from Texas who said "Yes, ma'am" and was getting bald.

In due time I'd break the engagement in a calm, beautifully written letter that would climax our correspondence and bring our romance to a tender close. "It is a far, far better thing that I do, than I have ever done" — that was Sidney Carton in *A Tale of Two Cities*, of course, not *Héloïse and Abélard*, but the general idea was the same.

By February I had Jim so mixed up in my mind with Abélard that I could hardly remember what he looked like. He wired, during midyear vacation, that he was making a quick trip North to see me. He had something important to ask me, he said.

What did he have to ask me? To marry him, probably. But why come all the way from Texas to Massachusetts? Why not ask me in a letter?

Suppose he asked me to marry him. What would I say? Suppose he asked me and I didn't hear him? Suppose — my heart thumped and my ears set up a loud sea-shell roaring — suppose he asked me some question and I wasn't sure whether it was about marrying him or not? What would I do? Pretend to feel nauseated? Say, "Wrinkelohwrinkelletdownyourhair?"

I certainly wasn't going to say, "Look, Jim, the reason I've got this blank expression on my face is that I'm not sure whether you just said, 'Let's go to a matinee' or 'Let's get married today.' "

I wired him I'd meet him in Boston. I didn't want to see him in my dormitory drawing room — a vast, Gothic-arched expanse of thick rugs and high-backed chairs where you and your date sat whispering for fear of being overheard by a near-by twosome. In Boston there would at least be taxicabs, hotel lobbies, and restaurants where there would be background noises to help me out.

On the train going to Boston I felt the familiar sickish little ball of panic in the pit of my stomach. I was sure I was coming down with a cold. I told myself I'd be all right. Goodness knows I looked all right. I had on my new caracul coat and I'd blown myself to an orchid. I'd borrowed Belle Cunningham's real pearl earrings and Anna Mary Dodge's twenty-dollar hat. Restez-vous.

But Boston in February was ice-locked, storm-bound, and sub-zero. Jim had never been North before. His warm Texas smile was pinched by New England cold. Boston awed him. His warm Texas personality was pinched by New England reserve. He was balder than I remembered, and I'd forgotten he had a small mustache. He said, "Howdy, Honey" and his Texas drawl was even lower than I'd feared.

Taxicabs were out of the question; the streets were sheeted in ice. Restaurants and hotel lobbies were empty and silent. Jim and I seemed to be almost the only two people alive. We went tea-dancing at the Copley Plaza. There were only a few other frozen couples in the huge ball-room. The chilblain-fingered orchestra didn't want to play.

I tried all my safety techniques, beginning with my teen-age list headed INTERMISSIONS, HOW TO COPE WITH. I delivered monologues, I dropped things. I had to telephone. I showed Jim match tricks; I choked and got hiccoughs; I read his palm. If it had been possible I would have reverted completely to boarding-school days, filled his mouth with large pieces of chewy candy, and started singing "Moonlight Bay."

Finally, in desperation, I invented a note to write. Jim followed me into the hotel writing room and pulled me down on a sofa beside him. We had to talk low; a porter was sweeping, a few feet away. Jim asked me something. The man had traveled two thousand miles to ask me something. To this day I don't know what he asked me.

I began to sneeze. I sat on the sofa in the writing room of the Copley Plaza shaking with chills and fever and sneezing my head off.

The next day my cold was virulent and my temperature a hundred and three. I said good-by to Jim over the telephone; I could hardly speak and there was no use trying to see him again.

"Write to me," I croaked hoarsely, and soon his letter came — his usual grand letter, tender and sprightly. Toward the end he said, "By the way, Honey, do I imagine it or do you have a little trouble with your hearing?"

I tore his letter in tiny, hateful pieces and lay in bed nursing my cold, erasing Jim Fisher from my mind. Jim Fisher didn't matter, I told myself. He could go to blazes. I'd never see him again. I'd never wanted to see him again anyhow. I hadn't liked him; I had only liked writing letters to him. He was an unglamorous bald Texas engineer with a small mustache. I'd never liked mustaches — not since I stopped loving my beloved Judge Hopkins at the St. Louis Trust Company. Drat mustaches. I'd write the next essay in my series about men with mustaches, I decided. I'd jeer at mustaches. I'd erase them from the earth. I'd say mustaches were a lot of silly nonsense.

5

"WANT to go along?" Anna Mary Dodge asked me one afternoon toward the end of Senior year.

We were walking across campus with half a dozen classmates. A freak April snow had fallen which padded footsteps and muffled sound; I had little idea what was being talked about.

"Sure," I agreed. Anna Mary's pretty pink-and-white face looked anticipatory — and hungry, as usual. She was a great athlete and got so much exercise that she was always starving to death. "When are you going?" I asked her, taking it for granted she was going to the Village Tea Room for fudge cake and hot chocolate with whipped cream.

"The Fourth of July. Do you mean it? Could you really go?"

"Of course." I knew now I had let myself in for more than a trip to the Village Tea Room. The other girls' faces registered respect and a flicker of envy; apparently this was something good. Oh, well. It was a great life. I was used to it. Before long I'd find out where I was going. Anna Mary would say, "Don't forget —

58

you're doing such-and-such with us over the Fourth." Hope it's a Fourth of July cruise, I said to myself. The Dodges lived in Cincinnati and had a motor boat. It was no motorboat cruise, though. I could have kicked myself for saying Yes so glibly, when I found out I was sailing to England on July Fourth on the Aquitania.

Her parents were delighted I was coming along, Anna Mary told me. They hoped I wouldn't mind spending all the time in England, which they must do, since Mr. Dodge was a delegate to the American Bar Association Convention in London. I minded very much. England would mean endless hush-hush cathedrals and art museums and dimly lighted historic spots; endless sight-seeing trips conducted by inaudible tourist guides. A Bar Association Convention would mean banquets with endless inaudible after-dinner speeches. Oh, well, I'd told Anna Mary I'd go. There was nothing for it but to follow through. It was a great life, but at least sight-seeing tours to Dickens's Old Curiosity Shop wouldn't be as dreary as botany walks and *Dryopteris filix-mas*.

Judge Hopkins would approve. This would be just about the last pretty little letter I'd have to write to the Judge. In a few months, praise be, I'd be of age and could spend my money without supervision. Aunt May and Aunt Harriet would not approve. They'd fuss and worry — certain I'd be murdered, or at least robbed, without them along to look after me. They'd make me a black sateen money pouch, such as they always wore when traveling, suspended from a belt and secured to the thigh with an elastic band. Furthermore, they'd make Mrs. Dodge promise on her honor to see to it that I actually wore the awful thing.

Poor aunts, they were worrying themselves sick about me. They couldn't believe I really didn't want to come home after college, as my sisters had done; that I really didn't want to be-

59

long to the Thursday Club, flutter in flowered chiffon at teas and Charity Guild benefits, and live for Saturday-night dances at the Country Club. They couldn't believe I really didn't want to marry a young man from a fine family and settle down, as my sisters had done, in a lovely home of my own. Specifically, they couldn't believe that eventually I wouldn't marry my teen-age beau, Roger Evans, who was still as good-looking as he was when we went to Dean Academy together and who still took me to dances whenever I was at home.

The only way to convince the aunts was to get a job in the East — preferably a job on a newspaper. Armed with the essays an editor of the *Atlantic Monthly* had praised, I had gone to Hartfield, a small city not far from Boston, to be interviewed by the managing editor of the *Hartfield Register*. He hadn't been interested in my essays (the *Atlantic* editor had just praised them; he hadn't published them) but he told me his society editor was taking a leave of absence in the fall and I could have her job if I liked.

He introduced me to the city editor, Mr. Morgan, who would be my boss. Mr. Morgan's desk stood in the middle of a city room noisy enough to make bedlam envious; he himself had the voice of a train announcer. I met Mr. Stone, the star reporter, who was a year out of Harvard and looked interesting, and Mr. Keith, the music critic, who looked admiring and said, "Hel-lo! Welcome to the newspaper world."

I was tickled. I'd be safe in the newspaper world — in all that din of typewriters, telephones, and teletype machines. I wouldn't be a silly society editor long, either. I saw myself with a Press badge, the center of all the shouting at fires, accidents, riots, national political conventions. I saw myself in a Press chair smack against the witness stand, covering murder, kidnaping, and other outstanding trials. I saw myself at the theatre, in the first-row center of the orchestra, looking the spit and image of a dramatic critic.

My job was to start in October. Meanwhile I'd go to England with the Dodges. On this first trip I'd learn the ropes of foreign travel. My next trip — to Vienna and Dr. Abraham Leopold, of course — would be made alone.

No one was to know about my second trip. I didn't want a lot of family discussion and speculation about where I was going and why. Simply — one day I'd be off, cotton in my ears. Months later I would return, hearing the grass grow.

In imagination I ran into old friends.

"My dear, welcome back! You're looking divine. Those clothes — Paris, of course — Molyneux? Patou?"

"Chanel. But do you mind speaking a trifle lower, my dear? These Midwestern voices. . . after living abroad. . . quite deafening. . . ."

"I'm going to Vienna about a year from now," I told Dr. Richardson when I went in to see him for the last time. "I'm going to get my hearing fixed up by Dr. Leopold."

"He might help you." Dr. Richardson nodded. "Nothing to stop you from trying him out, certainly. Leopold is unique, no question about it. Unfortunate that he is unique, because, like all of us, he's not getting younger every day." He shoved the round mirror back from his forehead. "Got a husband picked out for yourself, have you?"

"Nope. I'm not going to get married till I get my hearing fixed up."

"Not worried about having hard-of-hearing children, are you? You needn't be. No reason to suppose a tendency to your kind of progressive deafness is inherited. Your own hearing might go down a bit with pregnancy, that's all." He clapped me on the shoulder. "You go right ahead and get married," he rumbled. "And don't be afraid to have childen. Have all the children you please."

I hadn't thought of children. It was in-laws I was afraid of. Not that Roger Evans's mother scared me. She was rosy-faced and easygoing as Aunt May and very fond of me. Possibly she even knew my hearing was below par. If she did, she'd be loyal; she'd never in the world let on she knew it. I sometimes suspected definitely that Roger's sister Rita knew. Rita didn't raise her voice but she had a way of clearing her throat a little pointedly before she spoke to me that made me wish for Wrinkel. Wrinkel always killed people off for me who cleared their throats pointedly.

Dr. Richardson asked, "Ever think of studying lip reading?"

"Heaven forbid." I shuddered. "We've got a girl in my class in college who reads lips. She gives me the willies."

He tilted his chair. "You may not have a miracle in Vienna, you know."

"Yes I will," I assured him.

This was my last appointment. Dr. Richardson shook hands as I was leaving. I noticed the deep grooves in his face and how far back his nice gray eyes were under his shaggy white eyebrows. As he'd said, he wasn't getting younger every day.

"Good-by, little boy." He smiled. I had bobbed my hair that spring, and I had on a black velvet jacket, a round, starched Peter Pan collar, and a knitted black silk four-in-hand tie. We all wore flat heels and Peter Pan collars and looked like little boys that year.

Dr. Richardson put a hand under my chin and tipped my face up to see it better. "You'll make a lip reader," he said. "You've got the eyes for it — good, alive eyes. Don't put it off too long."

I looked at his thick snow-white hair and remembered how, Sophomore year, I'd planned to marry him and minister to him faithfully during the closing years of his life. "Don't put it off too long," he repeated, giving my ear an affectionate pinch. He was such a nice man. It wasn't until I was going down in the elevator that I wondered what it was I shouldn't put off too long. Getting married? He needn't worry. I wasn't planning to put off getting married. Only until I'd had my miracle in Vienna.

I wrote "Journalist" firmly in the space after "Occupation" when I applied for my passport to England. I hunted up a Certificate of Newspaper Credentials I had had since I was fourteen. This was an item I had seen advertised in a magazine; you sent one dollar to a P. O. Box somewhere in Kansas and by return mail received a printed card bearing your full name and address and instructions that you were entitled everywhere to all courtesies customarily extended to the press.

Looking for the certificate, I came across a deck of fortune-telling cards that had stood me in good stead a couple of years before at Belle Cunningham's Hunt Week house party. Ocean travel, being a fresh experience, would present me with fresh acoustic hazards, I knew. The Aquitania would hardly be as hush-hush as the horsy Maryland house party, where everyone talked in such high-bred undertones that, though I was no horsewoman, I had contemplated riding and falling off on my head, just for the pleasure of hearing some good loud screams. But neither would the Aquitania be so enjoyably rackety as last summer's train observation platform, where I had heard everything Jim Fisher said without trying.

I put the fortune-telling cards in my suitcase for luck, though actually I wasn't worried about this trip. The Dodges were friendly people — self-assured and hearty. I'd be all right if I remembered two things. First, to be nice, so everyone would like me. Second, to look alert, interested, and appreciative, so everyone would think I heard everything that was being said.

Our crossing was rough. The three Dodges were poor sailors. I might have been a poor sailor, myself, except for Mr. Flyte, a tall, thin British teakwood merchant with a huge bony nose and a plaid woolen muffler. Both tireless deck walkers, he and I bumped each other so regularly the first day out that it seemed safer to join up and walk in the same direction.

From my point of view, Mr. Flyte had everything against him. His voice was low, his accent very British; his lips never moved, nor did the muscles of his face. On deck he kept his mouth buried in three folds of muffler; indoors he kept a pipe between his teeth. But I was glad I had him. You needed a man on shipboard. With hail-fellow Anna Mary around to help me keep conversation spirited, I would naturally have gone gunning among the sons of Dartmouth, Princeton, or New Haven, all well represented.

But Anna May lay light-green in our stateroom. I was on my own. Mr. Flyte walked me around the heaving open deck where the wild wind tore and the bitter spray stung and told me long, involved anecdotes of tigers, teakwood, and his years in India. I could hardly understand a word he said, but I was very nice and looked alert, interested, and appreciative. He liked me, though I baffled him sometimes.

Whenever I felt greenish, Mr. Flyte took me to the smoking room for a whisky and soda. I was perfectly safe in the smoking room. I had done very little drinking in my life so far, and I now made the congenial discovery that drinking made people's speech fuzzy and it was all right to say "What?" That was the summer of the British Empire Exposition at Wembley, and a joke went the rounds which no one appreciated more than I did:

First drunk: "What station's thish?"

Second drunk: "Wembley."

First drunk: "You're wrong, ol' man — 's Thursday."

Second drunk: "Right. So am I, ol' man. Lesh get off right here and have a li'l drink."

Also, everyone said "What?" to Britishers. In our smoking-room circle, failure to cope with the British accent was called pulling a chauncey. This was because, one afternoon when spray lashed the portholes and the floor rose and fell and our highball glasses skated against the table racks, an American asked the smoking-room steward if he thought the sea would ever calm down.

The steward: "Chauncey is rocking the boat, sir."

Eventually it was agreed that what the steward really had said was, "The chawnces are rawther remote, sir."

Between alcoholic fuzziness and the British accent, the smoking room was full of mild, hilarious confusion about what was being said. All mistakes were funny. It carried me back to the days when I was six and was called a funny little monkey and could bring the house down by exclaiming, "Goodness gracious, I'm a radish!" I invented a chauncey story about my barging into the ship's engine room by mistake which compared favorably with my sidesplitting account, at the age of twelve, of how I happened to take Aunt Harriet's crochet pattern to Mrs. Schlee instead of to Mrs. McGee.

Ordinarily I would have died rather than own up to the engine-room incident. It was the kind of embarrassing blunder a hard-of-hearing person makes continually: I'd been trying to find the swimming pool and had misunderstood a steward's directions. I barged into the engine room and barged out again

65

like a shot, naturally. But that wasn't the way I told it in the smoking room.

The engine crew, stripped to the waist and coated with grease, had not welcomed me, I related. For a minute I hadn't been sure whether they were going to throw me out or throw me in a furnace. Fortunately I carried my handbag and in it my Certificate of Newspaper Credentials. A flash of my one-dollar Kansas open-sesame and they accepted me — without joy but as a journalist. I was allowed to stand and watch the engines. One wiry little oil-streaked wiper even let himself be interviewed — and this was the pay-off because of course he was pure British and as for understanding a word he said — well, the chawnces were rawther remote.

My favorite chauncey story concerned Mr. Flyte, whose anecdotes of India as we walked around the deck sounded something like this:

"Feller named Pippip. Sir Pip said, 'Oh, I say, Pippip, old wrink, you're not pippiping that pip with a pippippippip!"

In my mind's eye, I could see Sir Pip (stout, choleric, top hat, fancy weskit, monocle) and the feller named Pippip (thirtyish, sandy; bit of a bounder, obviously). Pippip was proposing to shoot a tiger with a bullet of the wrong caliber, I decided. Or dynamite a teakwood tree. . . I say, old wrink, really. Can't do that. What d'you expect, though? Feller's not a gentleman, what?. . . And who's saying who's not a gentleman? It's top hats and monocles makes gentlemen nowadays, is it? Sir Pip, is it? Ask him how he got that Sir. Him and his fancy weskit.

Sir Pip was indignant. His father was a baronet before him, he shouted. He got so red in the face I decided Pippip was probably righter than he knew. Sir Pip choked and the monocle fell out of his eye. I giggled. Mr. Flyte stared at me.

66

"Oh, well — it's a great life!" I exclaimed.

Mr. Flyte stopped walking, his big nose ruby-colored from the wind and his plaid muffler whistling straight ahead of him. He took his mouth from his muffler. He was baffled.

"But, I say," he protested. "The feller died, y'know!"

I told that story often in the smoking room. It was perfectly safe. Nobody else could understand what Mr. Flyte said, either.

"The first time I met you, I thought you were French," Princeton Peebles confided as we jolted to the Tower of London in an American Express Company motor coach.

Anna Mary and I had met Cornell Hoyt and Princeton Peebles at a tea given on the terrace of the Houses of Parliament for delegates to the American Bar Association Convention and their families. (Mr. Dodge had registered me as his niece.) We had looted a small French dress shop off Piccadilly for the occasion and wore suave, skillful little ensembles, Anna Mary's rose, mine powder-blue, that breathed Rue de la Paix.

"Our pink and blue outfits are a success," I told Anna Mary, who sat in the next seat of the motor coach with Cornell. "The first time Princeton saw us, he took it for granted we were French."

"Not Anna Mary. Just you," Princeton amended. "It's something about the way you listen."

"The way I listen?"

"Kind of like a French person who doesn't quite comprenez. It's cute. Mother noticed it, too. She thinks you're awfully attractive."

Princeton was an inadvertent conquest. He and Cornell were also in London with Bar Association elders; we were staying at the same hotel. Anna Mary and I scorned the two of them; they were moon-faced, still college undergraduates; between cathedrals and museums they gorged hot chocolate and pastry, which Anna Mary and I had given up in favor of the more sophisticated sherry and a biscuit.

Princeton's arm traveled behind my shoulders. "You know what?" he said. "I'm working on Dad to let me quit college when I finish next year. Law school takes too darned long. What the hell, I can get into insurance."

His moon face puckered. "You know what? I've been thinking. I might want to get married some of these days."

I smiled at him, secure in the hubbub of the American Express Company motor coach. American Express tours were tiresome but they had acoustic advantages. You were in a large, chattering group; the guides used small megaphones. I was so relaxed as we bumped across London Bridge that when Princeton asked me to wear his class ring I said absent-mindedly, "Okay, Wrinkelton, if you want me to."

My first day in London, the minute I had entered Westminster Abbey, I had thought of Wrinkel. I had thought of him many times since. What climbing he could have done, high in Westminster's soaring nave. How unconcernedly he would have tossed his rope ladder through a staple in the exact center of the vast dome of St. Paul's. How gleefully he would have straddled the little balconies above our hotel lobby, silently and mock-solemnly mimicking, "Good wrinking, Mrs. Wrinkles. Did you enjoy the wrinkit to Wrinkingham Palace?" "Not awfully, Mrs. McWrink. The wrink-and-wrinkney pie I had for lunch at Wrinkelmayer's beforehand gave me a touch of wracid wrinkagestion."

It may have been too much steak-and-kidney pie at Rumpelmayer's; it may have been London itself, heavy with centuries.

68

Whatever it was, most of our hearty, self-assured American lawyers and their families had lost their hearty self-assurance in London.

They tiptoed through our hotel lobby. They matched their voices to the discreet pianissimo of the hotel desk clerk's. In the dining room they whispered to waiters and to one another. When they gathered in groups in the hotel lounge for after-dinner coffee, they talked as if they were afraid of being shushed by Queen Victoria, who stood in marble in a nest of potted palms.

I had been avoiding the lounge after dinner, saying I had letters to write. It seemed a good idea, after the evening I had coffee there with Princeton and his parents. Judge Peebles asked if I'd like some crème de menthe and I said, "No, only three weeks, I believe." I thought he'd asked me if I were staying in London for a month.

Mrs. Peebles was the kind of mother who would be quick to find something wrong with any girl her darling boy looked twice at. She was an erect, handsome woman who stood head and shoulders above the paunchy little Judge. I could hear her firmly laying down the law to him ". . . a girl with poor hearing . . . saddle himself for life . . ." She thought the sun rose and set in her darling boy.

But everything was all right, apparently. It hadn't occurred to the Peebles family I had cotton in my ears. With Cornell and Anna Mary and thirty other panting American Bar Association delegates, Princeton and I plodded over the green lawns and up and down the damp, narrow staircases of the Tower of London.

We blinked at the Crown Jewels. We snickered at the red-coated guards and the blue-and-red beefeaters. We stood in the

Bloody Tower where the two little princes were murdered, and on the site of the scaffold where Lady Jane Grey sighed and died.

It was a pleasant day. If Princeton's voice dropped away, I put on my French listening expression and said with a laugh, "Pardon?" Unconsciously, as one does when talking to a foreigner, Princeton raised his voice a bit.

The sight-seeing tour included the Temple, the National Gallery, Dickens' Old Curiosity Shop, Ye Olde Cheshire Inne, and a quick look at the Elgin Marbles and the rest of the British Museum. At the end of the day Anna Mary and Cornell were bushed but Princeton and I were bouncing. He and I spent so much time together during the next week that Mrs. Peebles got worried. Princeton was too young to get engaged, she told Mrs. Dodge; it was dangerous for him to see so much of a girl as attractive as I was. She whisked him off with her to visit relatives in Scotland.

She needn't have worried. Princeton couldn't have been safer. He and I rode all over London on the top of the omnibus. We watched Punch and Judy shows, explored Scotland Yard, Baker Street, Fleet Street, and Madame Tussaud's. Discovering we both liked Max Beerbohm, we lost ourselves for a whole afternoon in the maze of the London Underground, trying to find our way to No. 2, The Pines, in Putney, the scene of Beerbohm's beautiful essay on Swinburne.

We went only where there were crowds, noise, and plenty of light. Daylight lasts until ten in the evening in summer in London; we were back at the hotel by ten and did no dallying in the lounge or writing rooms. I was risking no repetition of the Jim Fisher–Copley Plaza incident. Besides, I didn't like moon-faced Princeton much, though I was tickled that his mother thought I was dangerous.

The caretaker who showed our group of Bar Association delegates through Carlyle House in Chelsea said that whoever aspired to literary fame should sit in the window seat on the first stair landing. It was Thomas Carlyle's favorite spot, she said, and "Many's the inspiration has been got by those who've sat there."

I sat down in the window seat. I was tired. Drat Thomas Carlyle. Drat Chelsea. Drat Oxford, Cambridge, Windsor Castle. Drat Stoke Poges, where the curfew tolled the knell of parting day. Drat the American Bar Association and its endless sight-seeing tours. Drat Anna Mary Dodge, who kept saying "ever so" this and "ever so" that and seemed to be developing a British accent.

Anna Mary was ever so infuriating. Oh — we had had some good times together, she and I — especially the time we spent drinking wine. We had chipped in on a book called How to Drink Wine, which told the correct wine to drink with each kind of food and the correct time of day to drink it. We sipped burgundy with red meat, sauterne with chicken and fish, chablis with oysters, champagne with dessert. Whether we felt like it or not, we drank hock at lunch time, sherry at tea time, port after the dinner savory with a walnut or two. We tried every wine in our book. Not even Madeira stumped us. Promptly at eleven o'clock one morning, wearing our pink and blue French ensembles for courage, we took empty and unready Rumpelmayer's by surprise by walking in and ordering two glasses of Madeira and a plate of little sandwiches. (Madeira, How to Drink Wine said, should be taken at eleven in the morning with little sandwiches.)

Those were good moments, but for the most part Anna Mary was infuriating. She had majored in art in college, and she

71

lingered forever at madonnas and stained-glass windows, a cultured expression on her pretty pink-and-white face, holding forth inaudibly in what I privately called her culture purr.

Next to art her passion was the Royal Family. She read palace chitchat in the newspapers and stood for hours waiting to catch a glimpse of Queen Mary. Or she had heard of a tearoom in the Duke of Somebody's Mews where someone said the Prince of Wales had once lunched. The place would be a renovated stable, lit sparingly by candles, so quaint it didn't have menus. I'd order at random from a pippippip waitress and pretend to listen to Anna Mary comparing Cornell Hoyt unfavorably with the Prince of Wales, wondering whether my hearing was getting worse or whether she really was developing a British accent.

Thomas Carlyle, the caretaker of his one-time house was telling us indulgently, had bad manners. He was grouchy and unpredictable and rude. "But who cares for good manners in a great writer?"

It gave me an idea. Why be so all-fired nice all the time? Why not be ever so rude for a change? Wasn't I going to be a writer? Didn't I have a newspaper job just ahead?

I began going alone around London, poised and journalistic, I and my one-dollar Certificate of Newspaper Credentials. Anna Mary was jealous. If only she had a job ahead, she grumbled. If only she could be free and independent, as I was, to go around having adventures.

I loitered at No. 10 Downing Street, and was rewarded by a glimpse of the Prime Minister. Paying tribute to the Peter Pan statue in Kensington Gardens, I saw a man who might well have been Sir James M. Barrie. I walked up to the bar in a pub in Hammersmith and ordered Guinness because I'd read it was the ruin and solace of London charwomen. It was dark, sickish stuff, but I forced it down, feeling every inch a roving journalist, smoking a Gold Flake cigarette. That was the first time in my life I ever smoked a cigarette in public, though, like all my friends, I had been smoking surreptitiously for several years. Just imagine Aunt May's and Aunt Harriet's faces if they could have seen me standing in a London pub drinking Guinness and smoking a cigarette! Judas Priest. I was so tickled that on the way home I stopped in a swank shop in Bond Street and bought myself a small pipe.

I went alone to the British Empire Exposition at Wembley — "Wondrous Wembley," the posters called it. In the Palace of Beauty, Cleopatra leaned forward, naked and gorgeous in her barge, and asked if I were American. She pronounced it Ameddican and at first I didn't understand her, so I shook my head. When I realized what she'd said, I remembered Princeton Peebles, powdered my nose, and tried to look as French as possible.

In the India Building a man in a turban sold me a small carved box for fifty shillings. I thought fifty seemed a lot and realized too late the Indian actually had said fifteen. I was always getting fifteen and fifty mixed up. Oh, well. No use trying to argue with an Indian.

In the Burma Building, where a gigantic teakwood Buddha reminded me of my shipboard crony, I made the mistake of smiling at a man who looked like Mr. Flyte. Discovering my mistake, I looked French again, reached for my Certificate of Newspaper Credentials, and ducked inside a door marked "Press."

I had all those adventures. But meanwhile Anna Mary, drat her, trailing tamely in the wake of the Bar Association, had first chance at Cecil Holmes.

Bar Association delegates were given a reception at the University of London. Cecil was there with his father, a University professor. Cecil himself was reading for the bar.

"You won't like him," Anna Mary reveled. "You don't like men with mustaches. Cecil has an ever so cunning little blond mustache."

I did like Cecil when I met him. He was fair and blue-eyed and bonny. He looked the way a Prince of Wales ought to look. Cecil's father knew the Dodge family, and soon Anna Mary and I were invited for a long week end at the Holmes family place in Devonshire.

"The week end will be all tennis and cycling and horseback riding," Anna Mary, the athlete, gloated. "Cecil and his friends are ever so keen on sports. I've told him you're not — that you're literary."

I was to spend the Devonshire week end browsing in the Holmes library, apparently. I was also to be ever so nice to the Holmes family. There was a teen-age sister, Daphne. There was Cecil's father, a widower. There was elderly Cousin Bea Holmes, who ran the household. Packing for Devonshire, I came across my deck of fortune-telling cards. Ever so prayerfully, I put them in my suitcase for luck.

I needed luck. Holmes House was old and big and dark. Architecturally it couldn't have been lovelier. Acoustically it couldn't have been worse. Anna Mary and I were in separate rooms, mine at the end of a long, thickly carpeted hall. I couldn't hear knocks or approaching footsteps, and maids were forever hovering — white-capped pippippips who ducked their heads and asked sudden questions about unpacking and pressing and baths and 'ot water and early morning tea.

Cousin Bea Holmes was one of those formidable elderly women who made me wish I were invisible; she looked as if she'd as soon snap my head off as not. I hoped Professor Holmes wouldn't have a mustache. He didn't. He had a full, bushy beard. I couldn't understand a word he said. I could barely understand the other house guests. Willie Carr was a mealy-mouth who talked as if he were utterly exhausted. His sister Daisy was a wide-eyed shybird if I ever saw one. Rex Miller and the Honorable Emily Trent made me feel all hands and feet.

The Honorable Emily was a tall, stunning girl with rangy grace and black hair with a proud white streak running through it. She was a natural horsewoman, Anna Mary told me. Her speech was clipped and resonant; she smoked constantly; she was shortsighted and carried a tortoise-shell eyeglass, which made her look at least a duchess. Rex Miller was her cousin, equally tall, equally stunning. The two of them matched, somehow. Rex was also an Honorable. He was an exciting man. He had a lame knee from Château-Thierry and Anna Mary warned me that Cecil said Rex drank rather a lot.

"What's an Honorable?" I asked Anna Mary.

"Goodness knows," she said. "I think they're descended from William the Conqueror or somebody."

The first evening the Honorable Emily put up her eyeglass to look at me. She was wearing black satin, cut casually; my flame-colored georgette, all right until that minute, felt like a ruffled pinafore. She asked me where in the States I came from; she pronounced it Mizzudah, like Miss Eunice Drake. Later in the evening Rex Miller took me out on the terrace, tipped my head back with his free hand (the other held a whisky and soda) and kissed me. I was so flustered I nearly fell over the balustrade backwards.

The next morning everyone except me came down to break-fast in riding clothes.

Cousin Bea Holmes looked out sharply from behind the tall silver coffee urn.

"D'you write?" she snapped at me.

I jumped a little. She had taken no notice of me the evening before. I'd hoped she might never see me.

"Why, yes, I do — a little," I confessed.

"Oh, what fun!" crowed Cecil's young sister Daphne. She was fair and sunny as Cecil and talked in a lilting upward crescendo, the way a young rooster crows. "Cecil, d'you hear that? She rides! She *isn't* just clevah! She rides!"

Anna Mary looked surprised.

My heart thumped to the floor. I opened my mouth but nothing came of it.

The Honorable Emily, perfect in herringbone tweed with a crisp white linen stock, put up her eyeglass.

Daphne was thrilled. She'd lend me everything, she declared. She'd love to; she was my size.

"Where've you ever ridden?" Anna Mary asked curiously, looking up from a hothouse peach she was sharing with Cecil. Everybody was looking at me — Rex, also perfect in herringbone tweed, Daisy and Willie Carr, Professor Holmes, who had marmalade on his beard, and Cousin Bea, who was now snaping the heads off a bunch of hothouse grapes.

"Oh — in the West." My voice was faint, coming from a long way off.

It was true I had ridden. I'd had a ride on a Shetland pony when I was seven. Pamela Jones and I had had our pictures taken, aged nine, riding a camel in Hot Springs, Arkansas. The summer I traveled West with the aunts I had gone on an overnight pack trip in Yellowstone Park with a dozen other tourists. Aunt Harriet had insisted on my going, and I hadn't done too badly, climbing over steep mountain trails on a

76

tourist-hardened pinto, holding my Western saddle by its horn.

I'd ride Old Nellie, Daphne decided. Nellie was a love, ever so gentle — a bit blind on her off side, remember. How ripping that I rode, after all. Daphne had been detailed, I gathered, to stay home and amuse the clevah American while the rest went riding. Her relief was enormous.

I'd be all right on Old Nellie, the groom promised when he mounted me. Steady as a 'obby 'orse, Old Nellie. Children rode her. He showed me how to hold my reins and told me the names of them. I had never ridden an English saddle, I explained. He rode around the paddock with me while the others were mounting, showing me how to grip with my knees and rise to Nellie's gentle trot. I was all right. I was tickled. I lowered my chin and pulled in my elbows as I saw Rex and Emily doing. Who's a horsewoman? I asked myself.

Who's so Honorable? I grinned inwardly, untangling bridle from snaffle from pinkie, following the others out of the paddock. On the road I gripped with my knees and rose to the trot, imitating the two superb herringbone tweed backs I could see up ahead. Who's so Honorable? Them and their fancy jackets. Honorable, my eye, I was giggling to myself when an automobile passed Nellie on her blind side.

The car startled Nellie. I didn't hear it coming in time to pull her up. She reared and bolted. I went off her like a shot, landed smack against a stone wall, and knew no more. I knew nothing until I came to in my bed at Holmes House, smelling highly of ether and wearing a turban of bandages.

I wasn't much hurt. My head had needed a few stitches, that was all. I spent the rest of the week end in bed, wearing Daphne's frilliest bed jacket. Everyone, even the hovering maids, spoke up quite clearly when they talked to me. No one thought it odd I didn't hear well through such thick bandages.

I got out my fortune-telling cards and dealt Willie Carr hearts and the jack of diamonds (romance and a legacy ahead). He brightened and began to play a harmonica. His sister Daisy lost some of her shyness when I read her a future in small diamonds and clubs (travel on water and a letter bringing good news).

Cousin Bea said I had psychic insight. She brought Professor Holmes to my bedside for his fortune and I predicted high scholastic honor; Daphne had told me he was in line for an ever so special honorary degree. Daphne herself (whose continual lilting chatter about everyone supplied the whole of my psychic insight) circled my bed, crowing, "Clevah!" whenever I said something about somebody that happened to be true.

I dealt Cecil a row of hearts. He was a darling — full of compunction for my spill. I got awfully fond of him. He and Daphne improvised parties, bringing in their friends from around the countryside. It rained a lot and was too wet for much tennis, cycling, and horseback riding, anyway. Everyone gathered in my room to drink tea or ginger beer, while I told fortunes and Willie Carr tootled his harmonica and Anna Mary fidgeted. I'd ruined Anna Mary's week end, of course. I don't know why she was so furious at me for snagging Cecil. He married the Honorable Emily Trent the following winter; it was apparent that week end that that was what his family expected him to do.

Rex Miller and Emily Trent got poor fortunes. Spades are unlucky and, try as I would, I couldn't deal Rex and Emily anything much except spades. Ordinarily when that happened I ignored the cards and invented rich, glowing fortunes out of thin air, but I was tongue-tied with Rex and Emily. Rex sat taking long pulls at his whisky and soda, looking at me through half-closed eyes. Emily was chain-smoking, as usual. Every now and then she'd clear her throat before she spoke to me.

Pointedly? I didn't know. Every now and then she and Rex would look at each other and smile. What did they find so amusing?

Anna Mary was furious. You'd think I'd ridden Nellie and got myself thrown on purpose to break up her romance. I was furious, myself. I hadn't had to fall off Nellie. I was no horse-woman, but Nellie was steady as a 'obby 'orse; children rode her. I could have stuck on.

I hadn't wanted to break up Anna Mary's romance, either, believe it or not. But if I hadn't cracked my head falling off Nellie I'd have done it some other way. I'd have cracked it falling over the balustrade on the terrace. Or falling off a dining-room chair. There was a jinx on me that week end. The jinx was Rex and Emily.

What did Rex and Emily find so amusing? Were those two Honorables amused at me? Were they? I knew perfectly well they weren't — yet I kept asking myself: Were they secretly amused at me? Did they suspect I had mistaken "D'you ride?" for "D'you write?" Did they suspect why?

My heart skittered, even though I was safe for the rest of my stay at Holmes House, wearing soundproof head bandages, surrounded by reassuring noise. Blast Rex and Emily.

I'd ridden horseback that morning because I'd decided to ride horseback, I told myself furiously. No other reason. I hadn't been trapped into anything. I'd understood the question perfectly well. Oh, maybe I'd got rattled for a minute there at the breakfast table when Cousin Bea Holmes snapped at me suddenly with her sharp tongue and her British accent. Anybody could get rattled by a British accent. But I certainly knew the difference between "D'you ride?" and "D'you write?" What did those two silly Honorables think I was — hard of hearing?

6

WHEN I get to Hartfield, I promised myself, I'll have my own apartment. I'll have a living room so small and furniture so strategically arranged that no one can possibly sit too far away for me to hear. I'll have plenty of footstools; you can sit near people unobtrusively on footstools. I'll have plenty of lamps to liven the faces of deadpans; I'll have a victrola to keep mealymouths' voices up. I'll have my own doorbell and when shybirds ring I won't answer. I'll have my own telephone and when a lazydog calls up to ask for a date I'll say I already have a date with a quick brown fox. I don't like deadpans and mealymouths and shybirds and lazydogs.

"You're going to like this," the superintendent said, unlocking the door of a furnished apartment on one of Hartfield's good old elm-shaded streets.

I liked the house. It was mellow New England red brick, remodeled, three stories high, with two apartments to a floor. I liked the apartment — first-floor front, two small rooms, kitchenette, and bath. The furniture was passable; I could rearrange it strategically. I'd like the two girls who lived in the rear apartment on my floor, the superintendent told me. Quiet business girls, very friendly.

The first evening after I moved in it occurred to me to find my doorbell and put a card in it. Exploring the street entry, I saw a card on one side of the first floor button marked "Blake–Alger — Ring Once." The two quiet, friendly business girls, obviously.

Holding the door open, I rang the first-floor bell. It rang in the outside hall, between my apartment and the rear one. The latch on the street door buzzed. Two heads popped like twin cuckoos from the door of the first-floor rear. One red head, one overcooked yellow permanent wave. There was only one bell for each floor of the house, they explained shyly. Ring Once was for them, Ring Twice would be for me.

My heart sank. The bell seemed fairly loud, but would I be able to hear it inside my apartment? Would I be able to tell Ring Once from Ring Twice? Perhaps I wasn't going to like my new apartment after all. Certainly I wasn't going to like the quiet, friendly business girls. They were too quiet.

Friendly, they fluttered into my living room and perched shyly on my new footstools. Yellow Cuckoo exclaimed shyly over my new lamps. Red Cuckoo exclaimed shyly over my victrola.

"Do you smoke?" I asked them, offering my carved Wembley box of cigarettes. They drew back, visibly shocked. It gave me an outrageous idea. I picked up my Bond Street pipe from the mantel.

"Then I don't suppose," I laughed, "that either of you could lend me a pipeful of Bull Durham?"

First thing in the morning I'd get a tin of pipe tobacco, I

promised myself. What's more, I'd learn to smoke my pipe if it choked me, and let Red and Yellow Cuckoo see me doing it. That ought to shock them to death, I reasoned. That ought to frighten them away. Sorry, I don't like shybirds, I said to them silently.

"Sorry, I don't like you," I said silently to Lazydog Charlie Stone, the *Hartfield Register's* star reporter.

Lazydogs were different from deadpans, who were born that way; from mealymouths, who didn't know any better; from shybirds, who couldn't help themselves. Lazydogs were attractive men with plenty to say and good strong voices, who simply wouldn't bother to speak up. I had taken a course in typewriting at a St. Louis business school when I got back from England that summer. Like everyone who takes a typing course I had sat forever and ever writing "The quick brown fox jumps over the lazy dog." It tickled me to think of all the quick brown foxes in the world jumping over all the lazydogs, forever and ever — especially over Charlie Stone, the most sweet and maddening lazydog I'd ever seen.

Charlie was a native of Hartfield. His father was Dr. Cyrus Stone, head of Hartfield Memorial Hospital, and his mother was president of Hartfield's tony Fortnightly Club, prominent at literary teas and charity benefits. Charlie wrote color stories with human interest pull that got him by-lines in the *Register*. He did book reviews for Al Cummings, the *Register's* literary critic, who was a former *New York World* man and a good friend of Franklin P. Adams, conductor of the famous *World* column "The Conning Tower." Like every other young would-be writer in the East in the early 1920's, including myself, Charlie wanted to work on the *New York World*. Al Cummings said Charlie might make the grade. He said Charlie was a slow coach, but admitted he could write.

Charlie was long and lean with crisp yellow hair cut short to hide the wave in it. He went around, Harvard fashion, in an old torn raincoat, baggy slacks, a beat-up felt hat, and very clean blue shirts. He'd lounge into a chair beside my desk, fiddle with a handful of paper clips, grin a sweet, lazy grin, edge around to asking for a date. It was all I could do to hear him, even when the city room was noisiest.

When he stopped at my desk, therefore, I was brisk and busy. When we met at the water cooler I was preoccupied. Once when we met in the morgue and he started to ask for a date, I glanced at my watch, said, "Goodness!" and hurried away. That evening when he telephoned me at home I told him I was going to a concert with Allen Keith, the *Register's* music critic. The next time Charlie phoned I said I was having dinner with the *Register's* chief copy editor, Phil Braley.

If it hadn't been for Allen Keith and Phil Braley, I'd have been fired from the *Register* my first week. I started as society editor in October, a month of many weddings. I had a daily average of twenty weddings to write up and a social column to assemble. I could type "Now is the time for all good men to come to the aid of the party" and "The quick brown fox jumps over the lazy dog" lickety-split, touch system, using all ten fingers. But the pressure of deadlines and the hurry-hurry in the thundering voice of Mr. Morgan, the city editor, put lead in my fingers. Keith wrote up my weddings for me, threading dexterously through garlands of smilax and inset medallions of Venetian rose-point lace over antique ivory satin. On the copy desk Phil Braley good-naturedly checked the names and addresses in my social items and pasted them up in the order of their importance.

Keith was a cheerful, egg-shaped man who looked like a toy that you wind up. I always felt that if he were wound up he

83

would play and sing beautifully. He took me to concerts, and during intermissions and all the way home he hummed themes and beat out rhythms on the back of my hand, proving to me that Tchaikovsky cribbed from Brahms, or maybe it was Sibelius. He'd squeeze my hand and leave me at my apartment door, still humming and beating time, hurrying back to the *Register* office to write his review.

I was in awe of Phil Braley. He was a Yale man — big, good-looking, black-haired, sophisticated, several years older than I was. He wore really good clothes, a remarkable thing at the *Register*, where Keith came to work in plus fours and a bow tie and Charlie Stone in the pullover sweater he'd worn through Harvard. Braley had his suits made in New York, Keith told me; Braley spent most week ends in New York; he knew all sorts of rich and famous and important people there, Keith said. Phil Braley was by far the most exciting man I'd ever seen — exciting as the Honorable Rex Miller in Devonshire, only more so. It never occurred to me that he would notice me, except to help me out with my copy the way he'd help anybody else in the office. When I bumped into him one day at the office water cooler and he asked me to have dinner with him, I was so flabbergasted I spilled ice water all over my chin.

Thank goodness for my London sophistication. Phil took me to Hartfield's glossiest restaurant and offered me a cigarette as a matter of course. He suggested cherrystones and broiled live lobster, remarking that he wished we lived in a civilized country and could have a good wine with the lobster. A cold, dry white wine, I agreed, and Phil nodded at me approvingly. Thank goodness for Anna Mary Dodge and our joint book, *How to Drink Wine*.

Thank goodness for my London powder-blue ensemble that

breathed Rue de la Paix. Phil nodded approvingly at it, telling me I looked more like an editor of the New York fashion magazine, *La Mode*, than like the society editor of the *Hartfield Register*. After dinner he took me to a speakeasy on a dark side street and we drank illegal imitation cognac ordered in double talk and served in demitasse cups. It was my first speakeasy and my first cognac, but I took it all as casually as Madeira and little sandwiches at London Rumpelmayer's at eleven o'clock in the morning, and I could see that Phil approved.

Phil had been abroad several times, and while we ate lobster in Hartfield he told me about lobster at Prunier's in Paris, about crepes Suzette at Foyot's, filet of sole at the Marguery, pressed duck at the Tour d'Argent. He told me that the chestnut trees turn yellow very early in summer along the Champs Elysées and that it is pleasant to take a river boat up the Seine to Chantilly and go tea-dancing at the Pavillion Bleu. He told me about onion soup at Les Halles at dawn and about the tiny street near Notre Dame called the Street of the Cat Who Fishes. He told me about talking to the dean of American expatriates, Ezra Pound, at the café du Dôme, and meeting James Joyce and Gertrude Stein at Sylvia Beach's bookshop, Shakespeare & Company.

I told Phil I wanted to be a writer and he nodded approvingly. "Go ahead. Maybe a good-looking woman can be a good writer. It's a nice idea."

Phil knew everything about writing. He lived at a hotel in Hartfield and you could hardly get inside his room, Keith told me, it was so full of books and magazines. Literary reviews and foreign periodicals. Books by James Joyce and Thomas Mann and Marcel Proust — authors I'd never heard of in college English class. Phil never wrote anything himself. He sat "in the slot" — at the head of the *Register's* copy desk, taking other people's stories over the phone, editing other people's copy with his blue pencil.

I'd been aware of his voice since my first day on the *Register*. He never talked loudly, but his voice had a carrying quality. I could hear it without trying, though the copy desk was clear across the city room from my society desk. I'd hear him on the phone, taking a story, saying, "Yes. . . All right. . . All right. . . Okay. . . Yes. . . Right. . ." at regular intervals. His voice was a great comfort. I wished there were more voices like it on the *Register*.

Jean Parks, the librarian in charge of the morgue, was such a pippippip you'd think she'd been raised in England, not New England. A pale, brittle spinster, marooned among yellowing envelopes of clippings and old bound files of the *Register*, Jean was herself a storehouse of vital statistics. She was always pippiping that Mrs. Pippippip was in the hospital and I never knew whether Mrs. Pippippip had a heart attack or a new baby and whether to look glad or sad. The morgue was a dim spot, anyway, far from the safe, noisy city room. Everyone spoke low automatically; it was like a public library, only worse. I'd have avoided the place if I could, but I had to check my social file against the obituary file; Mr. Morgan, the city editor, had raised Cain the time my column carried an item about a woman who had been dead some time.

The *Register's* staff cartoonist, Weatherlow, was a mealy-mouth. He gave me fidgets. He thought me worldly because of my London clothes and often perched on the edge of my desk, an oily, cadaverous man in loud-colored shirts and hard collars, mouthing sly undertones, telling me "good ones" on all the members of the *Register* staff. His attention was flattering but I wished he'd go away. He ferreted out everyone's secrets. What

86

if he discovered mine? That would be a good one. Weatherlow had a fund of good ones on dear old Mannie Dixon, our staff photographer, who had a face like a half-opened clam and was so deaf he couldn't hear thunder — or couldn't hear organ music, at any rate. A Weatherlow cartoon captioned, "Hear Comes the Bride?" hung over the city editor's desk, commemorating the immortal occasion on which Mannie, unaware that the organ was pealing the march from *Lohengrin,* had walked down the church aisle at a large Hartfield society wedding carrying camera and tripod, a few feet in advance of the bridal party.

The *Register's* social column was graded, items about important people at the top. Only mid-column and bottom-of-the-column items were likely to come in from outside. I had to telephone for top-of-the-column cream.

A card file on my desk held the names, addresses, and phone numbers of all socially interesting families in Hartfield. Each morning I called a dozen or so matrons listed on these cards, hoping to catch them in good humor, asking if they had any social news. The cards had been annotated by generations of society editors before me. Notations ran like this:

"Nice. Call any time."

"Don't call. Her sister, Mrs. Brooks, will tell you about her."

"Good source, but unreliable. Better check."

"Deaf, but hears well on the phone. Call often."

The last was Miss Nellie Dennis. I never saw Miss Dennis, but during the nine months I spent as society editor of the *Register* I talked with her every few days. She lived alone and passed her time telephoning. Her flat, shrill voice reminded me of Mrs. George Furness back home who used an ear trumpet and bore her affliction bravely. It also reminded me of wonderful Marge Martin, the hard-of-hearing girl in my class in

87

college. Miss Dennis wasn't wonderful, though. She didn't bear her affliction bravely. She hated it. She told me she was crazy as a loon, heaven knew, but she'd go completely crazy if she couldn't talk to people on the telephone. The telephone was her life line to the outside world.

"People make me so mad," she said. "They tell you there are lots worse things than deafness. What are they? That's what I'd like to know. I'd like somebody to name me one worse thing. Blindness? Blind people can sit and talk to their friends. Lameness? Lame people can forget all about being lame for hours at a time, sitting and listening to music. Try to forget about being deaf," she challenged. "You can't, even when you're alone. You keep listening for the doorbell or wondering if the phone rang. Reading or sewing or playing solitaire, you're listening to the roaring in your ears. You're a prisoner, in solitary confinement."

She had a houseful of ear trumpets and electric hearing-aid contraptions, Miss Dennis said, but they weren't powerful enough; she couldn't hear with anything as well as she heard over the phone. Lip reading wasn't much help; she was nearsighted. She hardly ever went out any more. "People don't like to be seen with a deaf person. Makes 'em feel too conspicuous. Not that I blame 'em," she said, "but it makes me mad to see them pointing to their ears when they think I'm not looking and exchanging little sly smiles over my mistakes."

One day Miss Dennis told me about the time when she was a young woman in her twenties and turned up in evening clothes at a picnic because "We have two guests" sounded like "We'll have to dress." She lost her best beau that night, she said. He didn't know she was hard of hearing; naturally he thought she was a fool, wearing chiffon to the beach.

"After that," she said, laughing, "people told me to face
88

reality and admit I didn't hear. So I did. Do you think that made my friends speak up? For a few minutes. Then they'd forget or get impatient and go back to mumbling among themselves."

She'd been arrested in 1918, she told me, walking along the waterfront at New London, Connecticut, carrying one of the new portable electric hearing aids. She carried it in a square black box the size of a large camera; the receiver was a black disk the size of a biscuit held over her ear by a metal head-band. She looked like a telephone girl or a wireless operator, Miss Dennis said. Naturally the Shore Patrol arrested her. New London was an important submarine base; they thought she might be an enemy spy.

"People tell you nobody ever dies of deafness," she snorted. "That's nonsense. You do die of it, spiritually. A dozen little deaths a day."

I knew what she meant.

Mr. Morgan, the city editor, thundered at me, purple-faced, one day. He despised mistakes and didn't think much of women, either. "You responsible for this?" he demanded. It was a review of a concert Allen Keith had dictated to me over the phone. Keith had a hangover and after all he'd done for me I was glad of a chance to help him out. The review stated that the orchestra leader conducted "with all the brilliance of a house committee." What Keith had said, of course, was "with all the brilliance of a Toscanini."

A Hartfield society matron, top-of-the-column, whose card in my file read "Handle with gloves," was indignant because I laughed heartily when she told me her daughter was going abroad to study, for a change. What she'd said, I realized a moment after she'd hung up, was "study for the stage."

Charlie Stone's mother telephoned laughingly to protest that

89

the Fortnightly Club's guest of honor was an authority on pedigreed dogs, not pedigreed hogs. Must be my Missouri background, I laughed. Mrs. Stone said she did so want to meet me. Charlie had told her about my delightful sense of humor.

I covered a reception held at Hartfield Memorial Hospital for the opening of Dr. Cyrus Stone's pet project, the new Baby Clinic. Charlie's father was a darling — round and rosy as one of his babies, with kind eyes smiling behind shiny gold-rimmed spectacles.

"Come and see my babies," he invited, taking both my hands. "One hundred and thirty-eight of them, all singing 'How Dry I Am!' High time a pretty girl like you took interest in babies."

I died half a dozen of Miss Dennis' little deaths that day. The hospital office staff, from whom I needed to get names, facts, and figures, were deadpans. The Baby Clinic nurses, from whom I needed to get color stuff and anecdotes, had been trained, like all nurses, to speak low. Dr. Stone telephoned the next day to point out a few mistakes in my story — typographical errors, the darling called them. He knew enough never to blame a newspaper reporter for typographical errors, he assured me. Didn't he have a reporter right in his own family?

"Come and see us," he urged warmly. "Mrs. Stone and I both want to know you. We hear a lot about you."

The next Sunday afternoon Charlie asked me to go to the movies with him and home for Sunday-night supper with his family. I went to the movies but I didn't go home with him afterward. I wasn't going to be such a chump. I wasn't afraid of Dr. Stone. He was such a darling, he'd pooh-pooh the whole business of hearing. He'd say Charlie was interested in a lovely girl, not in a pair of ears.

But I talked with Mrs. Stone regularly on the telephone about Fortnightly Club items. I didn't have to meet her. I knew her well. I'd been meeting her all my life. She was clear in my mind's eye — formidable as Aunt Harriet, erect and decisive as Princeton Peebles' mother devoted to her darling boy. Her high-pitched voice reminded me of Aunt Harriet's great friend, Mrs. Graham, Senior. I could still hear Mrs. Graham wailing, "Don't tell me, Harriet, my darling boy's going to saddle himself for life like poor, patient George Furness."

I wasn't going to meet Mrs. Stone until I'd been to Vienna and had my hearing fixed up. I was too devoted to her darling boy, myself. It was getting so I couldn't keep my mind on my work when Charlie was in the office. His desk was several rows ahead of mine and he usually lounged with his feet on it, the beat-up felt hat on the back of his head, staring out the window, fiddling with a handful of paper clips. Charlie was the slowest writer on the *Register*. He'd stare and fiddle and kill time strolling over to the water cooler, stopping to talk baseball and prize fights or argue football prospects with the sports department. He was a great sports fan; I'd have to get to like sports, I told myself, after we were married. Also, Slow Coach Charlie would have to write a little faster after we were married, so we could afford to have babies enough to satisfy Dr. Stone and send all the boys to Harvard.

Sitting at my desk, typing "Now is the time for all good men" to make the city editor think I was working, listening to Phil Braley's voice across the city room saying "Yes. . . All right. . . All right. . . Okay. . . Yes. . . Right. . ." as he took a story over the phone, I planned my life as young Mrs. Stone. I had a big, rambling, haphazard house and seven children. I didn't have much time for my own writing, but that was all right. I'd have time when the children were bigger. Or

Charlie could do the writing for both of us. Moreover, young Charlie, whom we called Chip, was awfully smart with his blocks; it was easy to see he was going to be literary when he grew up. One afternoon I sat like a moonstruck schoolgirl, typing "Mr. and Mrs. Charles Stone, Mr. and Mrs. Charles Stone," when Weatherlow, the oily cartoonist who went around collecting "good ones" on everybody, slid up behind my chair.

I jerked the page out of my machine in the nick of time. If Weatherlow had seen it, he would have had a good one on me. But Weatherlow already had a good one.

"You know what you ought to do?" he said. "You ought to get your ears examined. I said hello to you three times in the post office this noon and you didn't hear me."

My heart skittered, but I laughed. "I must have been dreaming of Paris." I had, in fact, been mailing a letter to Madame Dupont, my college professor. I had asked Madame the name of the pension in Paris she recommended. I was going to Paris that summer. Everybody was going to Paris that summer. Paris was marvelous, everybody said. The franc was down to six cents. Paris was simply marvelous.

I'd go to Paris, I told myself. I'd get some Paris clothes and stroll in the Tuileries. I'd see Montmartre and the Folies Bergères and have a champagne cocktail at the Ritz Bar. Then I'd go to Vienna and put myself in the hands of Dr. Abraham Leopold. High time I got my hearing fixed up. High time, as Dr. Stone had said, a pretty girl like me took interest in. . . Now is the time for all good men. . . Mr. and Mrs. Charles Stone. . .

Phil Braley, walking past my desk just then, nodded at me.

"I'm going to Paris this summer," I told him.

"Stay there until I save up some money and I'll join you," he said.

"Will you really? Will you roll hoops in Luxembourg Garden?

"I'm better at rolling my eyes."

"Will you drink absinthe and carry a cane?"

"I'll eat snails," he promised.

"Will you bring your merciless editorial blue pencil and draw a mustache on the Winged Victory of Samothrace?"

I had shown Phil the essays I wrote in college and he made short work of them with his blue pencil. He went through my bookcase, too, and threw out J. M. Barrie, Christopher Morley, Donn Byrne, and H. H. Munro. He left me Max Beerbohm. "He's all right if you want a little man to wear in your buttonhole," Phil conceded.

I worked at home in the evenings, writing articles I hoped to publish in the *Atlantic Monthly, Harper's, Scribner's,* and the new *American Mercury.* Every week or so Phil dropped in, whipped out his blue pencil, and riddled to bits everything I had written.

"Look," he told me, when he had me in protesting tears, "you don't have to be a writer. God knows why you think you want to be one. Writing is a dog's life. You wouldn't catch me at it — not if the ghost of Shakespeare himself offered to stand at my elbow and dictate a sequel to *Hamlet*. But if you're determined to write, make up your mind to one thing: writing is hard work."

If Charlie Stone telephoned when Phil was at my apartment, I'd tell him to come on over. I was safe with anyone, even Lazydog Charlie, when Phil was in the room. I could always

93

hear what Phil said and from that I'd get a clue to what the other person was saying. Moreover, for some inexplicable reason, Charlie, and all lazydogs for that matter, would speak up when there was a third person around.

When spring came, Phil and Charlie and I often met for dinner. After dinner we'd walk across Hartfield Bridge in the blue twilight and hang over the stone railing watching the evening sky darken, watching the town lights thicken, full of ourselves, full of what we wanted.

Phil had a favorite quotation: "Be careful what you want, because you are likely to get it."

The three of us didn't have to be careful. We knew what we wanted.

Charlie wanted to write a book that would be something like Samuel Butler's *The Way of All Flesh* and something like Somerset Maugham's *Of Human Bondage*. I wanted to write a book that would be something like Emily Brontë's *Wuthering Heights* and something like Max Beerbohm's *Zuleika Dobson*. Phil wanted to read both our books. He wanted to read them, he said, sitting in his glass-and-chromium New York apartment, surrounded by Picasso originals, small sculptures by Maillol and Despiau, rare first editions of the world's great books, first-rate recordings of the world's great music, Filipino house boys, orchids, champagne, and dancing girls. Phil wanted money. Pots of money. Lashings of money. He said money was the root of all good.

Arm in arm, the three of us would walk back to my apartment and drink bootleg gin mixed with ginger ale. We talked about writing. Phil taught Charlie and me, the writers, what good writing is — something neither of us had learned in college English class. Phil talked about Thomas Mann and Proust and James Joyce and sometimes read us passages from Joyce's

Ulysses. He actually owned a copy of *Ulysses;* he had smuggled it in, paper-covered, and had it bound regally in real leather. *Ulysses* was banned by censors in this country and published only by Shakespeare & Company in Paris. Young litterateurs who went abroad were smuggling the big paper-covered copies through the customs the way everyone was smuggling bottles of real cognac and crème de menthe and Scotch.

All three of us wanted to live in New York — Charlie and I because that was where the *New York World* was, Phil because New York had the best glass-and-chromium apartments, art, music, champagne, and dancing girls.

In May, Charlie left. He got a copywriting job in a New York advertising agency. You couldn't jump to the *World* from the *Hartfield Register,* he said. Thing to do was to go to New York, take any job to eat on, free-lance for the magazines, get yourself a name.

In July I sailed for Paris. I sailed from a booming New York, roaring with the 1924 Democratic National Convention. Charlie wangled passes and took me into the Press Section at Madison Square Garden. I spent two popeyed evenings in the thick of history in the making.

Bands blared. Delegates yelled and stamped and howled. They whistled and hooted and threw their hats in the air. They grabbed one another in snake dances and paraded around and around the Garden while Alabama repeatedly cast twenty-four votes for Oscar T. Underwood. A man with a full-toned voice, Franklin D. Roosevelt, stood up on crutches to salute New York's Governor Alfred E. Smith as "The Happy Warrior." Franklin P. Adams was in the Press Section and Charlie and I introduced ourselves to him. We stood talking about Al Cummings, literary critic on the *Hartfield Register,* whom F.P.A. knew well. I was so thrilled I could hardly breathe. I was ac-

95

tually standing in the Press Section at the Democratic National Convention in Madison Square Garden talking to the great F.P.A., conductor of "The Conning Tower" of the *New York World*. I told him I wanted to work on the *World*. He told me to come in to the *World* office to see him when I got back from abroad.

I had braved the Fifty-seventh Street shop of the swank dress designer, Maggie Rafferty, and spent a month's salary on a dress to travel in. It was navy-blue crepe, cut straight, with a demure white piqué collar and a shoulder-length cape lined in scarlet. With it went a navy-blue turban with a white cockade. I hoped to goodness I looked like a celebrity as I went up the gangplank of the Ile de France with Charlie. I felt like a celebrity. My cup ran over when, at the top of the gangplank, I distinctly heard one woman say to another, "Isn't that the Princess Bibesco?" She probably wasn't, but she seemed to be, looking straight at me.

Charlie asked me something or other. He was such a lazydog, and since he'd been in New York the sweet and maddening idiot had even grown a square blond mustache.

"What?" I said.

I'd been saying "What?" to him all evening. It was exciting and perfectly safe. The next time I saw Charlie I'd be hearing the grass grow. I was going to Paris. From Paris I'd go to Vienna. I had written to Dr. Richardson in Boston. He would work up a summary of my case history in German, Dr. Richardson wrote me, and send it to my Paris address, together with a letter of introduction to Dr. Leopold.

Next spring I'd be back in New York. Charlie would have his job on the *World* by then. I'd get a job on the *World* myself. When Charlie asked for a date I'd say Yes. If he asked if I loved him I'd say Yes. If he asked if I'd marry him —

96

He was asking something or other. . . if I'd send him a letter by the pilot boat. . . something or other. I didn't hear it but it didn't matter. Next time I saw Charlie I'd be hearing everything. I'd be cured. There'd be no more peril in the word "What?" No more panic, no more hiding, no more secrets, no more subterfuges, no more bluffing — nothing to be afraid of. No more enemies. No more shybirds, mealymouths, deadpans. No more lazydogs.

"So long, lazydog darling," I said, and kissed Charlie good-by quickly.

7

I WAS back in New York in four months. Paris was marvelous, but if I'd stayed longer I might very possibly have married a dear, dumb, devoted man named Ernest Goodfriend. I had to leave Paris to get away from him. There was no point in going to Vienna. No point whatever in going to Vienna. Soon after I arrived in Paris I had a letter from Dr. Richardson. Dr. Richardson was sorry — he didn't keep abreast of medical journals as well as he should these days. Checking up on the Vienna address he had learned that Dr. Abraham Leopold was dead.

I had picked up a handful of letters at the American Express Company that morning and walked across to the café de la Paix. Letters from the family. Letters from Charlie Stone. When was I coming back? Charlie wanted to know. I wasn't really planning to spend the winter in Paris, was I? I kept saying Paris was marvelous. What was so marvelous about it?

Well, for one marvelous thing, I could hear in Paris. It was just as I expected.

At the Maison Vitelle, the pension très, très, TRÈS comme il faut recommended by Madame Dupont, I could hear everyone. If I couldn't, I looked puzzled and said "Pardon?" — whereupon everyone smiled and repeated, raising their voices instinctively for the foreigner.

I was the only American. There were the three Mesdemoiselles D'Arcy — dark-eyed little sparrows who twittered in the corridor, buttoning one another down the back, hurrying to classes at the Sorbonne. There was Mademoiselle Felice, spinster sister-in-law of Madame Vitelle; she dyed her hair very black and patted and smoothed it while she chattered archly with Monsieur Paul. Monsieur Paul was a Sorbonne professor, always smiling, always springing to his feet and bowing.

Last, first, and always, there was Madame Vitelle. She was monumental, with many chins—a cross between a spoiled baby and Queen Victoria. She never went out. Stairs were beyond her and she'd grown too heavy for the lift. She ruled her world clamorously from the fancy little green-and-gold salon, enthroned in a huge armchair elaborately carved with cupids.

When she was in good humor, Madame tied a large red-satin bow to the collar of Rochefoucauld, her trained fox terrier, and put him through his tricks. Afterward she held him on a clean white towel spread over her black satin lap and rewarded him with pink and yellow bonbons.

When she was in bad humor, Madame pounded the floor of the salon with the stout walking stick of her late husband, booming violent orders and calling names. Pounding the rounded bottom of a carved cupid on the arm of her chair, she ordered the scurrying Mademoiselle Felice to march herself vite, vite, VITE to the butcher shop and invite the pig of a butcher to cut his throat. She boomed at the garçon who dashed around in a red-and-white-striped jacket, calling him robber, villain, fool. She ordered him vite, vite, VITE to drown himself.

There were no hovering maids, no soft knocks at Maison Vitelle. Every morning, when I rang my bell, the musical-comedy garçon burst through my door, put coffee and croissants on my bed table, and sang in an agreeable tenor, "Bon-jour-mad'moi-SELLE!" For lunch and dinner the pensionnaires gathered twittering and chattering at a large oval table with Madame Vitelle enthroned.

Madame Vitelle teased me about the slowness of my French. Rochefoucauld, she said, was much quicker than I to comprehend. Actually, my French was improving. My accent was better and I could understand the shrill, rapid put-put-put of table conversation fairly well — not instantly, perhaps, but if I waited and thought a minute the meaning might flash over me. I would beg Monsieur Paul or one of the Mesdemoiselles D'Arcy, "Attendez un moment — je vais comprendre." Madame laughed until her chins danced. She called me Mademoiselle Attendez.

Paris was marvelous, and it was full of familiar faces. My letter from Aunt May read, "We told Laura Foster to look you up. You remember Miss Laura — you were in her Sunday-school class. She is making a tour of England, Scotland, and France with her niece — trying to marry the girl off, as your Aunt Harriet says. We worry with you over there by yourself. It relieved our minds when Mrs. Graham, Senior, recognized the name of your pension. She was in Paris last summer and was made very ill on one occasion by drinking a small glass of wine. Do be careful. Call on Mrs. Jones. She will be in Paris (Hotel Crillon) in August on her way back from visiting your old friend Pamela in Rome. Pamela has a baby — a darling little boy. Her husband is that nice young architect who won the prize."

My two oldest sisters wrote reminding me of their glove sizes, their lingerie longings, and their children's favorite colors. My sister Ann wrote to be sure to look up So-and-So. "She knows Paris inside out and can give you lots of addresses."

There was little need to look people up. You ran into everybody — in hotel lobbies, on the street, calling for your mail. Everyone carried packages. There would be squeals and hellos. A dash for the nearest café. Tea or an apéritif. "Isn't Paris marvelous?" "Have you seen Connie?" "I bumped into Dot in Montmartre." "Isn't Paris marvelous?" Then the important question. The opened handbag. The search for the small leather-bound notebook. Addresses.

Addresses of linen shops, lace shops, glove shops, shops that made beaded bags to order. Out-of-the-way addresses — two flights up and down a hall. Little shops. Little novelty shops. Little millinery shops — "Ask for Yvonne; she's a genius; she was with Jean Patou for years." Little shops for matched lingerie, dirt-cheap, made to measure and exquisitely monogrammed. Little dress shops ("Say I sent you, of course") where pirated copies of couturier originals could be had — "for so little, my dear, it's all you can do to keep your face straight."

Paris was beautiful that summer of 1924. Paris had wonder and grace and charm, as usual. Paris had the Louvre, as usual, and Notre Dame, and jewel-like Sainte Chapelle. Paris had palaces, landmarks, and museums, treasures of history and art. Just outside were Versailles and Malmaison, as usual. Not too far away were Chartres and Amiens and Mont St. Michel, as usual. They had been there some time, and we all knew they were there. But the franc was down to six cents, and who knew when the franc would be down to six cents again?

I was tickled that nobody wanted to go sight-seeing, that nobody cared for cathedrals and museums. I'd had enough of inaudible tourist guides and hush-hush cathedrals and museums in England the summer before. I spent July and August shopping and sitting with my friends at sidewalk cafés. Swank, crowded cafés on the Right Bank; on the Left Bank, the teeming café du Dôme and café de la Rotonde. Big places. Noisy, well-lighted places. No dim little bistros where Poet So-and-So slapped his mistress. No quiet little basement dives where Composer Such-and-Such wrote his suite for woodwinds and violins. No atmosphere, please, in Paris. I'd had enough hush-hush atmosphere in England the summer before.

One day, as I stood in the mail line at the American Express, a familiar voice sang out, "Hey! You've improved! How are you? Do you still snore?"

Stella, of course — my roommate at Drake School. Pretty as an angel, full of lively concerns. She was married to John Fogg, son of New York's big music-publishing house. They were in Paris for the winter, living in an apartment off the Etoile with two grand pianos and so many mirrors that John kept bumping his head.

How was I? Stella repeated. What had I done to my figure? It wasn't bad. Did I still walk around the room with a book on my head?

I was glad to see Stella. September had come. I had helped my friends finish their shopping, drink a farewell champagne cocktail and get off, one by one, on the boat train to Cherbourg. How they envied me, staying in Paris. How they dreaded going home — how could they ever get their loot in without paying a fortune in duties? How much should they declare? Should they rumple their new Paris nighties, snip the labels off their Paris dresses? Each one was smuggling in a miniature bottle of cognac for her best beau. Would she have the nerve to face the customs inspector in New York with the bottle shoved down in her bra?

The tourist tide had ebbed. Paris was a French city now. At Stella Fogg's I met mostly French people — musicians usually. Parties were large; the Foggs knew so many musicians that one piano — or both — was usually in action. I could hear everything. If I couldn't, I apologized for my bad French and the French apologized for their bad English. Everybody made funny mistakes all the time and laughed constantly.

It was at the Foggs' in September that I met Mike Goodfriend.

"Hey! Here's Ernest Goodfriend, a fellow author for you!" Stella sang out.

We liked each other on sight. I liked his broad, untemperamental American face in the room full of gesticulating musicians and foreigners. I liked his short, turned-up nose and hulking big shoulders. He looked guileless and substantial — dear and a little bit dumb. I liked him. He liked me because I didn't bat an eye at his name.

"Skip my name, will you?" he said. I hadn't batted an eye because I'd taken it for granted I hadn't heard Stella correctly. No one could possibly be named Ernest Goodfriend. In Seattle, Washington, where he came from, Ernest Goodfriend stood for a whale of a fine lumber business — his dad's — he told me. "Skip it. People call me Mike."

I might have married him. He wouldn't have minded having a hard-of-hearing wife. He would have skipped it.

He had skipped his dad's lumber business. He wrote murder mysteries under the pen name "Michael West." None of your highbrow literature for him. Skip that stuff. None of your highbrow music for him, either, he said, turning his broad back on the young American composer, George Antheil, who was the Foggs' great friend and was just then at the piano, playing themes from his *Ballet Mécanique*.

Mike liked opera, he told me; he went all the time; he had a book called *How to Listen to Opera*. He looked at me hopefully, and I said I liked opera, too. He asked if I'd help him tackle some of these famous Paris restaurants and go to the opera. I said I had a book called *How and Where to Dine in Paris*.

We met often for vermouth at the café des Deux Magots and had dinner at a different famous restaurant before going to the opera. We had lobster at Prunier's, crepes Suzette at Foyot's, filet of sole at the Marguery, pressed duck at the Tour d'Argent. We went straight through the repertoires of both the Opéra and the Opéra Comique and always went afterward to the café Grande Royale because the headwaiter looked like Major Brasenose, the detective who solved all murder mysteries by Michael West. Portly and unsmiling—Mike's Major Brasenose was never known to smile — the headwaiter always conducted us impressively to a red plush fauteuil in the very center of the great, glittering gold-and-crystal room. Mike and I had fun together.

He was a mealymouth, but I could skip that, because we spent our time in gay, crowded places noisy enough to keep his voice up. He didn't talk much, anyhow; he liked to hear me talk. At the Grande Royale he would sip fine champagne while I spun a new chapter of my continuous murder mystery, *L'Affaire de la Tasse de Sang Froid*. This was not a mystery to be written. It was like folklore or Penelope's web, always in the making. That was the fun of it.

My victims were men of two kinds only. I ignored women,

though the Grande Royale was full of them, vivacious in their fetching toilettes du soir. Mercilessly, giving no quarter to a disarming smile, a well-cut tail coat, or benevolent old age, I singled out all those men in the restaurant who had beards or mustaches. I killed them all off. The patterns of my crimes were infinitely varied — subtle, devious, and sure. Major Brasenose — he was disguised as the headwaiter, of course — was hopelessly baffled. By the end of each night's chapter of *The Case of the Cup of Cold Blood* Mike was full of admiration for the resourcefulness of my imagination, and there was not a bearded or mustachioed monsieur alive in the place.

He and I would make a dandy team of collaborators, Mike declared. He sometimes dropped in at Maison Vitelle on Sunday afternoon, bringing me candy, books, and flowers. That was what you took to a girl in Seattle. He would sit in our fancy little salon, saying little, his broad body folded into a pale-green satin-and-gilt chair, while Monsieur Paul bowed and the Mesdemoiselles D'Arcy twittered and Mademoiselle Felice patted and smoothed her black hair, which I now knew was not dyed but a transformation.

Madame Vitelle made a fuss over Mike. She would send the garçon vite, vite vite for wine in small glasses and put Rochefoucauld through his tricks. Her chins lively with mirth, she would fondle the terrier on his towel in her lap, feeding him pink and yellow bonbons and telling Mike how much quicker to comprehend Rochefoucauld was than I was.

She teased me about Mike. He would make a comfortable husband, she declared. He was an innocent, that one; he'd see no further than the tip of his short turned-up nose. Madame Vitelle was a shrewd woman. When I left Maison Vitelle on a few hours' notice she wasn't surprised, and she didn't offer to refund one centime of the six months' room and board I had paid in advance, though I had been with her less than four months. I didn't ask for a refund. She was in bad humor. I could imagine what she'd do. She'd pound the floor of the salon with the walking stick of her late husband. She'd pound the cupids' bottoms on the arm of her chair. She'd call me pig, robber, villain, fool, and invite me vite, vite, vite to cut my throat and drown myself.

I'm sure she knew it was to get away from Mike that I left Paris so suddenly. She was still enthroned in the salon when I came in that last night. It was late; I'd been with Mike to the Opéra and the Grande Royale. I stopped at the salon door to say bonne nuit and tell Madame the lift was out of order. I knew the French phrase perfectly well; l'ascenseur ne se marchait pas every few days. But I couldn't think of the words.

Looking at Madame Vitelle, a vast, bizarre madonna in her carved chair with Rochefoucauld on his towel in her lap, I felt my eyes fill with tears. It flashed over me what Mike had just asked me in the downstairs foyer.

I had said good night quickly, as I always did in that dimly lighted spot. I stepped inside the lift and pushed the button. Nothing happened. I'd have to walk up. Mike asked me something — some routine question, I'd taken it for granted — could he call me tomorrow, probably. I said Yes and went on up the stairs.

Now, trying to recall the French phrase for "out of order," I recalled instead the happy, incredulous expression that had appeared on Mike's broad, upturned face when I said Yes. I'd done it again, I told myself. I'd let myself in for something. Like botany walks in boarding school. Like the trip to England with the Dodges.

I'd always said there was no use getting rattled at such times; the thing to do was follow through. But this was a Yes I couldn't

106

follow through on. Because I was no more in love with Mike than I was with Rochefoucauld, and it flashed over me that Mike had asked me to marry him.

My retreat from Paris the next day was memorable enough so that some years later, when I was experimenting with magazine fiction, I based a short story on it entitled "Candy, Books, and Flowers." In "Candy, Books, and Flowers" I called myself Kay. Mike Goodfriend was Derek Farnham, a successful lumberman.

The story opened with Derek Farnham arriving at Kay's Paris pension, his arms full of c, b, and f, the morning after she had said Yes to his proposal of marriage and left him standing happy and incredulous at the foot of the stairs.

Kay was gone. She had left a note saying, "Sorry, I can't marry you." It was because she loved beauty and couldn't marry a materialistic lumberman. Homeward bound, she found an idealistic young poet on board her boat. Kay loved the poet's deep voice reading aloud his poems about beauty and it wasn't until just before the boat docked that it slipped out that the poet was interested in her because he thought she had money. (She did.) Materialistic Derek Farnham looked good to Kay when she reached New York and found him standing at the foot of the gangplank, his arms full of guess what. (He had crossed on a faster boat.)

What I really did in Paris that next morning was to send Mike Goodfriend a note by pneumatique. I sent another to Stella and John Fogg. There was a long, lean, lazy, sweet, and maddening character named Charlie in New York, I explained to the Foggs, who hadn't written me a letter in three weeks. I thought I'd better go see why. I explained to Mike that I'd been called home suddenly. I didn't mention his proposal; I skipped it. So did he. I got an announcement of his marriage to a Seattle girl a year later. A year after that I saw a murder mystery on the lending-library shelf — *The Case of the Cup of Cold Blood*, by Michael West — and skipped it.

When I wrote my short story "Candy, Books, and Flowers," I used Mr. Vogel, my pot-bellied little fellow passenger on the Mauretania, to furnish a touch of comedy. Mr. Vogel became a dear but daffy old shipboard philosopher who gave my heroine, Kay, some magic powder he guaranteed would make men love her for herself, not just for her money.

Actually Mr. Vogel was a silk importer, neither dear nor daffy nor very old. I had a bad cold that October evening as I stood on the tender watching Cherbourg's lights dim and the lights of the waiting Mauretania brighten as we approached her. At the railing beside me, a pot-bellied little man blew a companionable nose into a big silk handkerchief and offered me his bottle of powder. You put a pinch of powder up each nostril, he directed. It was guaranteed to cure head colds.

The powder made me sneeze. Mr. Vogel gave me a brand-new silk handkerchief like his own and told me to keep it; he had yards and yards of beautiful silk in the hold. The powder did help me breathe. It was like magic, Mr. Vogel told me. A silk importer travels all over the world, he said, and can't take chances. He never traveled without a bottle of this head-cold powder.

I hardly saw Mr. Vogel during the crossing. I got over my cold and forgot him until, at the costume party the night before we landed in New York, he waddled up and asked me to dance.

That was a gala party. A Canadian golf player about my size lent me a pair of white linen knickers. I wore my black velvet jacket from college days, cut myself a lace collar out of white cardboard, and went as Little Lord Fauntleroy. I was surprised when Mr. Vogel asked me to dance. I signaled distress to the Canadian golf player and he cut in as soon as possible. Not soon enough, though. Mr. Vogel's short arms squeezed me. He asked me a question. I didn't hear the question but the general idea was clear. I said No, decidedly, and held my breath until the Canadian came to rescue me.

When Mr. Vogel dropped in at my stateroom late that night I was still in my Fauntleroy costume, mooning over a marconigram from Charlie Stone and wondering if Charlie loved me and if so why he hadn't written to me for three weeks. I had found the marconigram under my door. It said "MEETING BOAT LOVE CHARLIE."

Mr. Vogel seized my hands eagerly and began talking about yards and yards of beautiful silk in the hold. The amazed expression on my face stopped him; he could see there'd been some misunderstanding.

He went right away, and I went back to mooning over my four-word marconigram. I guess Mr. Vogel was a philosopher, like the man whose prototype he became in "Candy, Books, and Flowers." But I've often wondered what the question was that he asked me when he danced with me. The idea was clear. You'd think the right answer — that is, the answer guaranteed to keep him from dropping in at my stateroom late at night — would have been a decided No.

Maybe he asked if I'd mind if he dropped in at my stateroom. Maybe he asked if I had any particular aversion to being given yards and yards of beautiful silk. As he said himself, a silk importer travels all over the world and can't take chances. Maybe Mr. Vogel asked if I was married, or in love. Maybe he asked if I was a virgin. I'll never know.

8

I STEPPED from the Mauretania on four-inch heels, wearing a traffic-stopping beige velours turban and a brown-and-beige Paris ensemble. At Bonnet Sœurs, where I had had the ensemble made, the model was called Le Léopard. The beige kasha-cloth dress was fashioned like a tube, so tight I could hardly move; it might have been iced onto me by a confectioner. It reached my knees — and skirts were still longish in New York that winter.

Like everyone who came back from Paris in 1924, I was a smuggler. I had declared neither Le Léopard nor my other Paris dress, Le Dragon. Le Dragon was turned inside out and wadded into a corner of my trunk with the paper-covered copy of *Ulysses* I was smuggling in for Charlie. Shoved down inside my bra was the miniature bottle of cognac I was also smuggling in, like every girl who came back from Paris in 1924, for my best beau.

I was saying to myself, Meeting boat love charlie. . . Now is the time for all good men. . . All right. . . All right. . . Yes. . . Okay. . . Mr. and Mrs. Charles Stone. . . .

Waving to me at the pier were Mr. and Mrs. Charles Stone. Charlie had mentioned Margaret occasionally in his letters; they worked for the same advertising agency. Margaret was a fashion copywriter. She couldn't know much about fashion, Charlie said. She dressed like Old Scratch and was always taking off her hat and forgetting it. He sometimes killed an evening listening to the radio at her apartment; it was more comfortable than the Harvard Club, where he lived. Had to kill evenings somehow; no use trying to get any writing done in New York during the summer; too infernally hot. Thing to do was wait till fall, get a place of his own. Margaret was a good sort, he said — I'd like her.

I did like Margaret. She was as long and lean as Charlie, with straight brown shingled hair and direct, serious-minded hazel eyes. She and Charlie looked a lot alike, but Margaret was no lazydog. She was a quick brown fox if ever I saw one.

She and Charlie had fallen into the way of meeting for breakfast at a restaurant near their office, she told me. It was good for Charlie; unless someone kept tabs on him, he'd stroll into the office nearer noon than nine. One brisk autumn morning about three weeks before she had suggested that instead of going to the office they go down to City Hall and get married.

It had been a good bargain, Charlie grinned. He'd married Margaret to get a comfortable apartment. She'd married him to get him to work on time.

Margaret's tan polo coat needed pressing and her tan jersey dress hiked up in front, but she knew fashion. Her reaction to Le Léopard was more than satisfactory. She'd see Le Dragon when we got home, I whispered nervously as I unlocked my baggage in the customs shed and spread out declared articles for inspection.

Le Dragon was my evening dress — heavy black crepe, the entire front covered by a gorgeous twisting beaded green dragon with ruby eyes and red beaded fangs. As we waited for the custims inspector, I told Margaret about my fittings at Bonnet Sœurs, where, each time I appeared, sharp, ecstatic cries to Annette, the fitter, went up from tall, thin Mademoiselle Bonnet and her short, plump sister, Mademoiselle Irene.

"Annette — Le Léopard!" they would cry in unison. "Le Dragon, Annette! Voici Mademoiselle du Dragon et du Léopard!"

I was so scared, now that I had to face the customs inspector, that I wished I had declared Le Dragon. But turned inside out it looked the merest rag. I had snipped off the label and wrapped the dress around the copy of *Ulysses* and shoved it down in the shoe compartment of my trunk. What if the inspector found it? What if he found *Ulysses*? *Ulysses*, of course, was not dutiable; it was contraband, like the miniature bottle of cognac.

The inspector was incurious, though. He asked few questions, ignored my shoe compartment, and finished quickly, seeming a little amused. When the Stones and I were squared away from the pier and settled in a taxi, Margaret thrust an arm through mine and leaned back exploding with laughter.

"Hats off to Mademoiselle of the Dragon and of the Leopard," she chortled. "Charlie told me you had a way with you. I see now he was indulging in one of his understatements."

On my other side, Charlie put an arm through mine. "What did she do — bribe the customs inspector?" He had been off bribing porters at the time.

"Nothing so conspicuous." Margaret laughed. "He asked her

if she'd declared everything. She looked at the good, kind government gentleman and earnestly answered, 'No.' "

I had thought the inspector asked if I had anything else to declare, of course. Now that my smuggling was off my mind and I could relax, I gave each Stone a congratulatory kiss.

"As soon as I get him bound properly in real leather," I told them, "I'm giving you *Ulysses* for a wedding present."

"Speaking of *Ulysses*, who do you suppose is in New York now? Phil Braley," Charlie said. "He's been here since October. Copy editor on the weekly news magazine, *Trend*."

"Phil?"

Thank goodness. There was someone in New York, after all. Phil would like Le Léopard. Phil would thoroughly approve of Le Dragon. My spirits lifted. There was someone in New York it would be fun to dress up for, after all.

"Let's call him up," I said. Phil Braley was my favorite character, I told Margaret. He was big and nice and solid — the most grown-up man I'd ever known. He was handsome and sophisticated and black-haired and knew everything.

Bumping uptown in the taxi between Charlie and Margaret, I held on to the idea of Phil. Little by little I was realizing that Charlie was married. My sweet and maddening Slow Coach Charlie belonged to this other girl. All right. . . All right. . . The quick brown fox jumps over the lazy. . . Now is the time for all good men to come to the aid of the. . . Yes. . . .

I could see Phil Braley's well-brushed black head bent over the *Register's* copy desk, his editorial blue pencil waving. I could hear his voice saying Yes. . . All right. . . as he took a story over the phone.

"Let's call Phil up right away," I said to Charlie, blinking to keep tears from spilling over the edges of my eyes, knowing all of a sudden what I'd do with my miniature bottle of cognac. "I've brought Phil a present," I said.

"Now that I'm here," I told Phil, "I want to get a job on the New York World."

Phil nodded. "There can't be more than ten thousand other literary-minded young squirts in town expecting to land a job on the World. How are you going about it?"

"I'm going in to see Franklin P. Adams," I told him.

I did go in to see F.P.A. After all, he'd told me to come in to see him when I got back from abroad, when I met him at the Democratic National Convention the summer before. I went down to Park Row one sunny winter afternoon. I entered the Pulitzer Building, under the famous green and gold dome. I was wearing Le Léopard for courage. Inside my left glove was a new-minted penny Charlie Stone had given me for luck. Now that he was married, Charlie had decided not to get a job on the World himself. There was more money in advertising. Thing to do, he said, was to work at home evenings and week ends, free-lance for the magazines. Margaret had fixed up a corner of the living room in their apartment for him to work in, and he was always planning, as soon as he had more time, to settle down to some real writing.

As I rode up to the World office in the elevator I was saying to myself, All right. . . All right. . . trying to feel every inch a grownup, like Phil Braley. What was there to be afraid of? I asked myself. Suppose the New York World was an important newspaper. Suppose F.P.A. was a famous columnist. I'd met him last summer. He'd told me to come in. What was I afraid of — that I wouldn't hear what somebody said?

The elevator dumped me into a dingy reception room where several hard-shelled newspapermen sat reading newspapers with their hats on. I knew they were newspapermen because they looked like all the men I'd seen in the Press Section at Madison Square Garden.

I stood there, feeling every inch a child. My ears were roaring. I couldn't have heard a fire alarm at ten paces. It was like the awful moment years before when I stood tongue-tied at my gate with Roger Evans, wondering whether he had or had not asked me to the school dance.

A pug-nosed office boy sat with his feet on the reception desk. He was reading a tabloid but he put it aside to give me his rapt attention. He eyed me up and down with anticipation, undecided whether to squash me fast or have the fun of slowly pulling off my wings.

"Glubglubglubglubglub?" he challenged, his mouth comfortably filled with chewing gum.

I wanted to s-see Mr. F-f-franklin P. Adams, I said, stuttering the way I used to in fourth grade when Miss Tin Ear Jenks made me stand up and face the class. Nobody heard me. I didn't want anybody to hear me. I knew perfectly well what would happen if the gum-chewing office boy and the hard-shelled newspapermen in the *World* reception room heard me say I wanted to see F.P.A.

They'd stamp and howl. They'd whistle and hoot and throw their hats in the air. They'd grab one another in a snake dance, chanting, She wants to see Adams, just imagine. . . She wants to see Mr. F-franklin P. Adams, no less. . . Alabama casts twenty-four votes for Oscar T. Underwood and goodness gracious the sweet little shybird's come in here with meal in her mouth and cotton in her ears expecting to see nobody at all except the conductor of that famous newspaper column, "The Conning Tower"!

"Glubglubglubglubglub?" the office boy threatened eagerly.

He had decided. He was going to pull off my legs as well as my wings, and very slowly.

The elevator came back just then. The door stood open and I dived for it. I had to do something. I couldn't just stand there. If I'd stood there another minute longer I'd probably have reverted completely to childhood and said, "Wrinkelohwrinkelletdownyourhair!"

Everyone had been nice at the *World*, I reported to Charlie and Margaret and Phil that evening, but F.P.A. was out of town. It wouldn't have got me a job if I'd seen him, Margaret said in her forthright way. Anyhow, I belonged on a fashion magazine.

"Walk into *La Mode*," she said, "and let Le Léopard do the rest.

I did get a job on *La Mode*, the chic, exclusive monthly magazine dedicated exclusively to the subject of chic. But first I found myself an apartment.

I found it in a tall modern building on Washington Square. Like my Hartfield apartment, it had two small rooms, kitchenette, and bath. As I had in Hartfield, I grouped furniture strategically so no one would sit more than a few feet away from me. I had plenty of footstools and plenty of lamps to liven the faces of deadpans. I had not only a victrola, now, but a radio, to keep mealymouths' voices up. I had good loud doorbells and no nonsense about Ring Once and Ring Twice. This time, I told myself with satisfaction, I had thought of everything. But I hadn't thought of Poison.

Poison was the apartment-house doorman — a huge, pompous, Brooklyn-born master of ceremonies in white cotton gloves, a military cap with a chin strap, and mulberry-colored livery decked out with gold epaulettes and loops of gold braid. His name was Bert but he was Poison to me.

I hadn't lived in the apartment house a week before Poison was clearing his throat pointedly before he said good morning to me. He said it loudly, with fish mouths — "Good MORNan." He followed this with "Nice DAY," watching closely to make sure I caught it. I longed for Wrinkel. Wrinkel would have killed him off for me. I don't know how Poison discovered my secret so quickly. Probably his dad was deaf, like nauseous Victorine Parry's dad, out in Chicago. Probably Poison, like Victorine, could spot a deaf person anywhere.

He would ring my doorbell and shout, "LETTA fa ya," handing me my mail. He would deliver a package, shouting, "PACKage fa ya," making anyone who was standing in the hall jump nervously and stare at me. When a telegram or special delivery came, Poison would clump to my door after the messenger boy, to help make it clear with huge, pointing white-gloved forefinger and exaggerated fish mouths that I was to "SIGN fa it on tha dotted LINE."

He did this outa tha goodness of his heart, see. "Gotta pipe up fa tha dame in 8A," I could hear him say to the handyman, as he changed out of his uniform in the basement locker room or caught a quick smoke between elevator trips. "Gotta pipe up plenty fa that baby. Puts up a bluff, but I spotted her. My Old Man's deef — I can spot 'em."

His manner to me was offhand, implying there was nuttin to it: one dame'd have de shakes — annudder'd have a game leg — annudder'd be deef — it was all in da breaks. There was also a kind of connivance — "I ain't givin' ya away none, see." Naturally nothing was said, but Poison never bawled "PACKage" when there were guests in my living room. There were no

"EVENans" or "nice DAYS" when I went through the downstairs lobby with Phil. Poison was especially cagey about Phil. I could hear him telling the handyman knowingly, "What da boy friend don't know ain't hoitin him."

Wrinkel would have relished killing Poison off for me. It occurred to me to kill Poison off myself. I planned a magazine sketch which I thought of sending to the new weekly, *The New Yorker*. In my sketch a shy, elderly spinster named Miss Keete wandered by mistake into the basement of her apartment building and in the recesses of the furnace room came face to face with the man she feared most in all the world — the doorman.

He was standing before his locker changing from his uniform into street clothes. Stripped of his gaudy livery, he was paunchy and out of condition. He had silly thin shanks in long underwear. Stripped of his military cap, he had no hair to speak of. Stripped of his military chin-strap, he had no chin. His mouth looked odd. Stepping closer, Miss Keete saw that he had slipped out his store teeth to rest his gums.

It would have been fun to kill Poison off — to revenge myself with words as in other years I'd revenged myself by ridiculing botany walks, winter sports, men with mustaches, and other enemies. But I didn't do it. I never wrote the piece about the doorman. I was afraid to.

Suppose *The New Yorker* accepted it. Suppose the piece appeared in print. Poison would never read it; there wasn't a chance he knew how to read fine print. But someone might read it to him, or tell him about it.

I knew what would happen if Poison found out I'd killed him off. He'd kill me back.

He'd wait until some evening I was all done up in *Le Dragon*, sweeping through the downstairs lobby with Phil and with — oh, Franklin P. Adams and the Prince of Wales. Slyly, Poison would set a snare for me. He'd ask me some low-voiced question. Trapped, I'd say, "What?"

I could hear him clearing his throat resoundingly, see his fish mouth forming for the kill. I could hear him shout, thrusting home the Seven Deadly Words, triumphantly virulent in Brooklynese:

"Whatsa MATTah, huh? COTTON IN YA EARS?"

That winter I caught a bad cold and kept it for months. I couldn't hear thunder — or at any rate I couldn't hear the shybird hairdresser, the mealymouth clerks in the grocery store, the deadpan bank teller who insisted on making friendly small talk while he cashed my checks.

I went through a series of glubglub part-time maids before I found Poppy, a large, plush-upholstered Negro with a rich, plushy voice. Then I had to fire Poppy; I heard her telling the back elevator man he'd ought to speak up, her young lady didn't hear so good. Poppy was followed by a middle-aged Irish woman named Vera, and at last I was safe in my own home, thank goodness. Vera was hard of hearing herself. We played our game together. When Vera suggested peas for dinner and I ordered cheese instead, she never let on it wasn't cheese she'd wanted all along. When Ellen Pringle telephoned and Vera's note on the pad read "Miss Trinket called," I said Mrs. Pringle sounded exactly like Miss Trinket and, anyhow, people should learn to speak up in this world.

Ellen and Tom Pringle were Phil's best friends. Tom was a well-set-up, squash-playing young broker; he and Phil had roomed together at New Haven. Ellen was a tall, slim snow princess, very blond, very lovely, very athletic, very social, very sure of herself and of Phil. She and Phil had been engaged for a while during college years, but Ellen wasn't in love with him. It was simply that Ellen liked everything in twos.

She had two men and two houses — a Park Avenue penthouse and a place on Long Island that she'd inherited from her family. She had two children — Tommy and Jerry. She had two Scotch terriers — Black and White. Thank goodness for Black and White. The Pringles' Long Island house was like Holmes House in Devonshire — old and big and dark — thickly carpeted, full of hovering maids. Phil and I often spent week ends there, and I'd have been lost except that either Black or White was always in my room to bark when someone knocked.

I was certain no one — not even Phil — suspected my secret, but it was tough going some of the time. Phil took me to big parties, small parties, dinner and the theater and night clubs. I was all right at the theater. Phil liked first-row orchestra seats, bless him, for the same reason that he liked ring-side tables at night clubs and lovely snow-princess blondes — because they were showy and expensive and hard to get.

I was all right at big, noisy parties where people danced and drank a lot. Small parties were all right as long as I stayed near Phil. But there were theater intermissions. Sure as fate, I'd be stranded during a theater intermission with some meek little mealymouth with a mustache. There were dinner parties. Sure as fate, at dinner I'd be put next to some sweet little shybird who ducked his head nervously and mumbled as if he were afraid he might give himself away.

The devil of it was that, though I didn't like shybirds — that is to say, though I couldn't like them, because I couldn't like anyone I couldn't hear — I had a soft spot in my heart for shybirds, just the same. I guess that was because I was a shybird myself — especially among those of Phil's friends who were important and very well-informed and sat about for long hours after dinner parties, drinking highballs and settling world affairs.

I was impressed and respectful at such gatherings, but I'd have loved to have just one other shybird I could compare notes with, for the fun of it, to see what he was making out of world affairs. I guess it was because I wanted a shybird for a friend and couldn't have one, in real life, that I invented Mr. Wilcox that winter. Mr. Wilcox was a neat, pleasant little imaginary man with eyes that snapped alertly behind his shiny glasses when something interested him, and a habit of fiddling despondently with his eyebrows when he couldn't figure out what people were driving at.

Mr. Wilcox and I had a lot in common. For one thing, no one noticed us when there was important conversation going on. We didn't mind. We'd keep amused, watching people's faces, criticizing their clothes, make-up, hair-dos, mannerisms; making sense — and more often nonsense — of what they said. I felt less lonely at parties after I'd invented Wilcox. He was a close friend. He reminded me of Wrinkel — in fact, he was the kind of little man Wrinkel might have grown up to be.

When I got my job on *La Mode* I took Wilcox with me. I needed him, because no one noticed me at *La Mode*. I looked chic enough. I did my job well enough. But I worked in a large, rather quiet editorial room full of desks placed far apart. I couldn't join in general conversation; too often I wasn't sure what the conversation was about. And no one bothered to include me or single me out. No one except Mrs. Crummins, the managing editor, who hired me, seemed to be able to see me very well.

Mrs. Crummins was a honey. Like all *La Mode* editors, she was chic and beautiful. She had a small, piquant, three-cornered face, honey-colored hair, and honey-colored eyes, full of laughter.

"Jean Patou?" she asked, looking appreciatively at Le Léopard when I went in for my first interview.

"About quarter to three," I replied, glancing at my watch. Then I saw she had an accurate desk clock and that the laughter in her eyes was brimming over.

We both laughed. It seemed wonderfully funny that I'd mistaken Jean Patou for half-past two. I told her about the time on the *Hartfield Register* when I took a concert review over the telephone and thought "Toscanini" sounded like "house committee." She told me her family still teased her because as a child she solemnly called the Book of Exodus the Book of Extra Dust.

My job was to write picture captions using the word chic as often as possible. Bored with captions, lonely in a large room full of chic, upstage beauties who didn't seem to know I existed, I grew more and more fond of Wilcox. I began writing short sketches about him, letting him work out my grudges for me and revenge me on my enemies. In one sketch Wilcox went to a large party attended by many chic, upstage, and beautiful women, mimicked everything they said and did, and made monkeys of them. In another he dined out and made a monkey of his hostess, a full-bosomed, authoritative woman who was the spit and image of *La Mode's* editor-in-chief, Mrs. Cavendish.

Mrs. Cavendish had beautiful hair, a well-cherished chin line, and a different perfect hat almost every day. She spent at least six months of every year in Paris and was always bursting into little French phrases, sprinkling whatever she said liberally with "Mais, non!" and Mais, oui!" She was in the office almost every day of the six months I spent on *La Mode*; I heard indirectly that she liked my work. But she never acknowledged my presence. Maybe she never saw me. Maybe I really was invisible in that terrible place.

One day in staff meeting an editor brought up the subject of glasses. Readers wrote in constantly, she said, asking *La Mode* to suggest fashions for women who wore glasses.

Mrs. Cavendish drew herself erect. Her hat for that day had a gorgeous green-and-gold bird on it; the sweeping tail-feathers set off her marcelled hair and accented her well-molded chin.

"I want it distinctly understood," she said, "that *La Mode* is not interested in women who wear glasses. Mais, non!"

That was the day Mrs. Crummins, the managing editor, had suggested that she and I lunch together some time. I never saw Mrs. Crummins except at staff meetings; her office was some distance from mine. I was tickled when she noticed me. She was a honey. She knew I was alive. After staff meeting that day I passed her in the corridor, standing at the water cooler.

"Thirsty?" She smiled.

I shook my head. "Guess not."

It wasn't until mid-afternoon that it suddenly flashed over me that Mrs. Crummins had probably been asking if I'd have lunch with her on Thursday. My heart sank. What on earth would she think of me? She'd never ask me again. How could I possibly explain?

I might tell the truth, I said to myself. I might just tell the truth. I might go into Mrs. Crummins' office and say, "Look, I wasn't being rude intentionally. I want to lunch with you Thursday. I'd adore to lunch with you Thursday. The reason I said 'Guess not' was because I didn't hear what you said. I'm somewhat hard of hearing, you know."

However, I remembered *La Mode's* official editorial attitude toward women who wore glasses and saved myself from deadly danger in the nick of time. If *La Mode* was making a clean sweep of all hopelessly deteriorated women with less than twenty-twenty vision, it was easy to imagine what would happen if a low no-account like me was unmasked, right there on the staff, who dared have less than perfect hearing.

I'd be set out on the back porch steps, of course. With a paper pinned to the collar of my dress. A slip of paper on the little collar of my chic little dress. Marked "For the Charity Guild." Mais, oui!

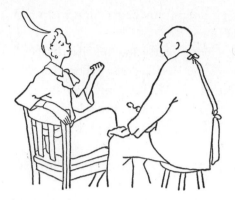

9

ONE fine autumn Saturday afternoon I walked along lower Fifth Avenue wearing a yellow wool suit, brown alligator shoes, and a brown skullcap with a long yellow quill in it. I was carrying a prescription which had just been given me by a man named Dr. Barnes.

The prescription had to be filled by a special pharmacist. It was non-refillable. Why non-refillable? Obviously because it would never require refilling. One filling would be enough. It would restore my hearing completely and for all time.

I stepped carefully over all the cracks in the sidewalk, as I used to do when I was six. Passing a churchyard that had an iron fence around it, I touched every other railing of the fence.

"Whoa, Junior," Phil Braley said when I bumped into him without seeing him.

"When I was six, back in Missouri," I told Phil, "we had lilac bushes in one corner of our yard. Every day, behind the lilac bushes, I closed my eyes and put my fingers in my ears and said 'wrinkelstiltskin' seven times."

Phil said, "New York is getting pretty low on lilac bushes."

He nodded at me approvingly. He liked my yellow suit and brown skullcap and alligator shoes. He liked my hair shingled close to my head. Ever since I'd had it cut that way he had been calling me Junior. He often asked me nowadays when I was going to marry him.

"You look like Dapper Dan himself," he said. "When are you going to marry me?"

It was September. I had resigned from *La Mode*. I had sold my first piece — it was about my imaginary little man, Mr. Wilcox — to *The New Yorker*. I had sold a long article in my high-pitched Max Beerbohm manner to *Scribner's* magazine. I was a writer now.

You needed good ears to be a writer, I discovered. Magazine editors spoke low. The editor at *Scribner's* was a distinguished deadpan with a full beard. The *New Yorker* editor who bought my Wilcox piece was a darling little shybird a lot like Wilcox himself. He took me to the Algonquin for lunch and ate straight through a plateful of creamed finnan haddie, which he said he loathed, rather than raise his voice to summon the waiter and get creamed sweetbreads, which was what he had ordered. He was very tired, he said. He'd been interviewing a writer all morning. The writer had had an idea for a *New Yorker* article. The idea had been horrible. The writer had been horrible. In fact, the man must have been stone-deaf. He'd had to repeat everything he said.

He shivered. "It was horrible. Finally I shut my eyes and hoped."

"Hoped?"

"Hoped he'd go away. And he did."

126

Yes, you needed good ears to be a writer. In fact, you needed good ears. That was the long and short of it. I'd been needing good ears for quite a while now — been needing them about as far back as I could remember.

I had written to Dr. Richardson in Boston, asking him to recommend a New York otologist. Meanwhile, on this fine autumn Saturday afternoon, I went in to see Dr. Barnes, who had an office not far from my apartment building and occasionally treated me for colds. I asked him whether he could do anything to improve my hearing. He was surprised that there was anything wrong with it.

"You oughtn't to be deaf," he protested. "Not with those eyebrows."

"Eyebrows?"

"Women with heavy eyebrows don't usually get deaf. Here, let me give you a prescription. You've got no business being deaf — a young woman like you — all her life ahead of her."

"Deafness is for old ladies," I agreed, recalling Dr. Dexter, the buoyant young Boston chiropractor. "Hey? What say?"

"Exactly," Dr. Barnes said with a laugh. "Now, you have to go to a special pharmacist for these capsules. Prescription's non-refillable. Take the bottle as directed and come back."

Hearing the grass grow? I stepped along carefully, going home from Dr. Barnes' office, avoiding all the cracks in the sidewalk, carrying my special, non-refillable prescription. Dr. Barnes was right. I had no business being deaf. His capsules would restore my hearing completely and for all time. If they didn't it would not be Dr. Barnes' fault. It would be because I had the wrong eyebrows. Or it would be because New Yorkers didn't have enough fences to touch in a special way when you passed by. Or it would be because, as Phil said, New York was getting pretty low on lilac bushes.

"When are you going to marry me?" Phil asked.

"What will you do with me if I marry you?"

"Stand you on the corner of the mantelpiece."

"Will you keep me shined up? Will you tie a blue ribbon bow around my neck on my birthday and a red one on Christmas?"

"And a red, white, and blue one on Fourth of July," he promised.

"In that case I might settle for the corner of the mantelpiece," I told him, "although I don't mind saying that I once planned to discover electricity, like Benjamin Franklin, and have my statue, life-size, in the park. I might marry you, though I don't mind saying that I once planned to marry a glamorous young violinist who pursued me through a moonlit rose garden wearing white tie and tails. I forget what I had on, myself. Sequins or cloth of gold, I think."

I might marry Phil, I thought. He was handsome and nice and by far the most exciting man I'd ever known. Marrying Phil wouldn't be at all like marrying Charlie Stone and living in a rambling, haphazard house with seven children and no time for my writing.

Married to Phil, I'd live in a stylish glass-and-chromium Park Avenue apartment and have plenty of time for my writing. Phil thoroughly approved of my being a writer. The trouble with most women writers, he said, was that they dressed like ragbags and forgot to wash. He liked the idea of a smart mind in a smart body, of polished prose written with polished fingernails. He still edited my copy with his merciless blue pencil and lectured me on writing the way he'd lectured Charlie Stone and me in the old days in Hartfield.

Phil had lost interest in Charlie. The Stones were having a baby and moving out to a house in Connecticut. Now, at last, he'd have time for his writing, Charlie was saying. No use trying

128

to work evenings and week ends in a crowded New York apartment. Thing to do was get a place in the country where you'd have some room.

Phil said Charlie had turned into that perennial bore, the potential author. The successful advertising man who kids himself that if the weather had been cooler, if the apartment had been bigger, if he hadn't married the girl he did, if the kids hadn't come along when they did, if he'd had more time . . .

Given all the time in the world, Phil said, Charlie would never have time for his writing. Given all the room in the world, Charlie would simply use it to raise alibis on a big scale. Soon he'd have a whole garden of alibis to relax in comfortably for the rest of his days. Phil said Charlie was lucky.

"Why?" I asked him.

"Because he'll never have to beat his brains out discovering that writing is hard work; that it's a complicated craft which, even at its worst, demands skill of no mean order. Because he'll never discover what is probably the truth — that he has nothing to say."

Yes, I'd dearly love to marry Phil, I told myself. He was big and solid and grown up and knew everything. Being married to him would be fun. I'd need good ears for that.

Married to Phil, I'd have to be grown up, as he was. Phil wouldn't want a wife who lived in a world of daydreams and fantasies and played silly games with herself about swinging on imaginary rope ladders and killing people off invisibly with deadly words. Phil was an important man. He wouldn't want a child for a wife — not even a dear, sweet, lovely child like me.

He'd want a poised, responsible woman — a clever hostess, giving parties, presiding at the dinner table — a credit to him in the presence of his friends. A credit to him, especially, in the presence of his old friend and ex-fiancée, Snow Princess Ellen Pringle, who liked everything in twos and was used to having Phil for her extra man. I'd need good ears to hold my own with Ellen Pringle — to say nothing of all the other tall, beautiful snow princesses in all the world forever and ever. Phil was an important and desirable man.

Married to Phil, it wouldn't be enough just to be well-dressed, so everyone would admire me. It wouldn't be enough just to be nice, so everyone would like me. It wouldn't be enough just to look alert, interested, and appreciative, so everyone would think I heard everything everybody said.

I'd need to hear what everybody said. I'd need to hear salespeople, servants, doormen, and elevator men. I'd need to hear the bid at bridge, the point of the anecdote, the murmured request for two lumps and lemon at tea. Moreover, I'd need to hear the drip of the leaky faucet, the miss in the motorcar engine, the bang of the loose shutter. I'd need to hear knocks and footsteps and whispers — the phone ring and the kettle boil over and the baby cry.

The thing to do was to get my hearing restored. Dr. Barnes' non-refillable prescription didn't restore it. Dr. Barnes said that was because I had so many colds that the capsules didn't have a chance. He referred me to a well-known Fifth Avenue practitioner, Dr. Dettridge, who was curing deafness by a special kind of finger manipulation of the Eustachian tubes. Dr. Dettridge could cure me, Dr. Barnes said. I had no business being deaf. Not with my eyebrows.

Dr. Dettridge had a lavish office, a cheerful, convincing manner, and a smile like a lighthouse, flashing off and on. He was fantastically busy, and so was his lavish waiting room, jammed with patients of all ages — all deaf, all cheerful, all having their deafness cured. I think Dr. Dettridge believed he could cure deafness. He told me that he was curing it every day, every hour, every minute. He showed me magazine articles and newspaper clippings. The articles carried pictures of Dr. Dettridge, close-ups of his "miraculous fingers," and drawings of Eustachian tubes before and after finger manipulation. The clippings reported sensational cures. Dr. Dettridge, according to these reports, had cured many celebrities, even European royalty.

He could cure me in six months, Dr. Dettridge told me flatly, if I'd give up smoking, stop having head colds, and come in five afternoons a week for treatment. My cure would cost fifteen hundred dollars. He laid the words flatly and matter-of-factly on the line — like that. My cure. My cure.

My cure. The sidewalks were full of cracks that afternoon, as I walked downtown from his office, and I avoided none of them. I didn't need to. I passed fences; for all I know I may have passed lilac bushes. It didn't matter. I was going to be cured now.

I knew that Dr. Dettridge was not an otologist. I suspected that he might not even be a bona fide doctor. I knew that bona fide doctors didn't show prospective patients newspaper clippings about themselves. I had been to some of the finest otologists in the country and I knew that they didn't think in terms of cures, much less promise them. I didn't care. Dr. Dettridge had stated flatly that he could cure me in six months. Was I going to do anything except believe him? Was I? Was I?

What was I? A young woman of twenty-four with all her life ahead of her and no business being deaf. A young woman with lovely, rich, full, exciting grown-up life just within reach. A young woman who had lived since early childhood in an invisible prison, longing passionately for freedom — for freedom from fear — freedom from fear of rejection, ridicule, failure.

From fear of people, fear of new situations, of real or imagined slights, awkwardness, embarrassment, mortification, misunderstanding, mistakes. Fear of loss. Fear of loss, above all. Loss of self-confidence, self-respect, self-esteem; loss of the confidence, respect, and esteem of others. Loss of the one thing, the only thing — the only thing that counts, the thing you die without. Loss of love.

Was I going to do anything except believe that Dr. Dettridge could cure me in six months? When he stated flatly that he could cure me in six months? Was I?

I went up Fifth Avenue five afternoons a week to have Dr. Dettridge put a rubber-gloved finger far back in my throat and do something to my Eustachian tubes. I gave up smoking. At the least sign of a cold I went to East Sixty-eighth Street to Dr. Harvey Graystone, New York's outstanding otologist, to whom I'd been referred by Dr. Richardson of Boston. Needless to say, I never let East Sixty-eighth Street know what Fifth Avenue was doing, or vice versa.

Dr. Graystone painted my throat and treated my sinuses. He gave me iron pills and calcium pills and phosphate tablets and sent me to have my wisdom teeth X-rayed. He tested my hearing with earphones attached to a pure-tone audiometer; the result was a graph on a chart something like a stock market report — an audiogram. Dr. Graystone scowled over my audiogram as if it really were a market report and he were losing money.

He was a kind, scolding, bald-headed, elderly little man. It made him mad that he couldn't do something to arrest progressive deafness when he'd spent all his life trying to do something to arrest it. The devil of it was that otologists still didn't know much about progressive deafness, he'd scold. It wasn't a question of curing it. Cures would be found someday, but that day was a long time off. Meanwhile you did wish you could keep your patients' hearing from getting any worse.

Most normally hearing people thought impaired hearing was kind of funny, Dr. Graystone fumed. It was funny at times, of course. Caused a lot of amusing mistakes. But impaired hearing was no joke. He'd spent his life treating people with impaired hearing, and he knew it was no joke.

More and more, life has become a matter of response to auditory stimuli, he pointed out. To get an education, to earn a living, to be informed, amused, diverted — even to keep from getting run over on the street — you depended on hearing. Man is a social animal; civilized life is based on the interplay of human relationships, which are largely a matter of verbal communication. Disturb a person's relationships with other people, Dr. Graystone said, and you create profound emotional and psychological disturbances. Withdrawal, despondency, isolation, hostility, brooding. Suicidal depression, not infrequently.

"Normally hearing people don't realize what the hard-of-hearing are up against," he said. "They take hearing for granted, themselves, and are unaware of the degree to which impaired hearing invades the dignity, undermines the personality, and drains the living spirit of a person. They think hard-of-hearing people are queer and difficult. Sometimes I wish every normally hearing person would stuff cotton in his ears and go about his business for twenty-four hours. He'd find he was beginning to act a little queer and difficult, himself."

Confident as I was that I myself was being cured right then, right over on Fifth Avenue, I enjoyed talking to Dr. Graystone about impaired hearing.

"You're a lot more cheerful than most of my patients," he said to me one day. "What's your secret? Got a nice beau?"

133

I nodded. I did have a nice beau, though that wasn't my secret.

"Does he know you're hard of hearing?"

"I'm not sure," I answered truthfully. It was perfectly possible that Phil knew I didn't hear well. On the other hand I always heard what he said without trying. I honestly didn't know whether he knew or not.

"Better tell him," Dr. Graystone said. "You'll feel guilty, marrying him, unless you do. Lord knows why, but there's a guilt feeling attached to poor hearing. You don't want to marry and live in dread of the time your husband will find out you've got bum ears. Tell him. Talk about it. It's always better to face reality."

I couldn't help giggling, thinking of Phil facing reality. Phil never faced reality. That was one of the most attractive things about him. Phil said reality was a snag-toothed hag, very dry and very cold. Far better to face a very dry, very cold Martini.

"You know, you ought to be studying lip reading," Dr. Graystone said, tilting back in his chair and putting the tips of his fingers together. "You'll make a good lip reader. Probably been reading lips unconsciously most of your life."

"Heaven forbid," I said with a smile, thinking of Marge Martin, the hard-of-hearing girl in college who gave me the willies, thinking how Phil would love having a spooky lip reader around. How about a spot of mind-reading along with it? he'd inquire. Did I know other tricks? Could I write with my toes? Walk on my hands?

"You know," Dr. Graystone said reflectively, a month or two later, "I think you might consider the possibility of getting one of the new electric hearing aids."

I snorted out loud. I couldn't help it. Judas Priest. Just imagine me — the well-dressed girl, Phil's Dapper Dan — rigged up in an electric hearing aid. Like nauseous Victorine Parry's dad, out in Chicago. Like Miss Nellie Dennis of Hartfield, carrying her transmitter and batteries in a square black box, getting arrested during the war as an enemy spy.

Suddenly I recalled the first electric hearing aid I'd ever been aware of.

"When I was six," I said to Dr. Graystone, "there was a deaf lady named Mrs. George Furness who kept an electric earphone in her pew in our church. I didn't know it was electric; I thought the earphone was connected with God. One day I went into the empty church and sneaked a listen, hoping to hear God say something."

He leaned back in his chair. "Did you know, at that age, that your hearing was below par?"

"I don't think I knew what hearing or not hearing was, exactly. I gathered that there was something the matter, that I wasn't as perfect as my sister Ann — the one just above me. That if I wasn't very careful to conceal my imperfection my aunts might send me away to the Charity Guild. They were always sending no-account things to the Charity Guild."

"Both your parents were dead?"

I nodded.

"They'd been 'sent away,' eh?"

"I guess that was it. The words 'dead' and 'deaf' sounded very much alike to me. I was always getting the two of them mixed up."

Dr. Graystone said, "You know, I think you'd get good results with a hearing aid. Not everyone does, by a long shot. But you have the right type and degree of deafness."

I felt like saying, "Oh, dryopteris!" The little man was hipped on hearing aids, apparently. I'd have been furious at him, but

135

I had just come from Dr. Dettridge's office and I felt fine. Dr. Dettridge was pleased with my progress, he told me. He thought my cure would probably take somewhat longer than six months because, in spite of his warning, I had had several bad colds. But there was no doubt in his mind, he said, that eventually my cure would be complete.

So I could afford to be amused at Dr. Graystone. He meant well. After Dr. Dettridge had cured me, I told myself, I'd come in some time and ask Dr. Graystone, quite casually, to test my hearing. I could see him scowling at my new audiogram, which would show normal hearing, of course. He'd think his audiometer was out of order; my hearing couldn't be normal. When he realized that it was, he'd be flabbergasted.

"Hearing aids are improving all the time," Dr. Graystone said. "They're getting smaller and lighter. You don't have to carry around a black box any more. You can wear the instrument right on you. A woman wears the transmitter fastened to her brassiere and the battery in a cloth carrying-case strapped to her thigh with an elastic band. The newest receiver is a disk small enough to be hidden under a woman's hair."

"Really?" I laughed. This was getting a little bit silly. What was the man trying to do — lose me my beau?

How Phil would love having a girl around who had a hearing-aid receiver hidden in her hair. Phil particularly liked my hair shingled close so he could rumple it. "Whoa, Junior," I could hear him saying, when he came across my hidden hearing-aid receiver. "What in hell's bells have we here?"

Just imagine me going around with a hearing-aid battery strapped to my thigh. Shades of the black sateen money pouch Aunt May and Aunt Harriet insisted on my wearing, the first time I went abroad. Just imagine me going around wearing a hearing-aid transmitter shoved down inside my bra. Shades of the miniature bottle of cognac I'd smuggled in from Paris.

How Phil would love me if I turned into a walking telephone. He said telephones were noisy and unsightly; he wouldn't have one in plain sight among the small sculptures and Chinese bronzes in his stylish glass-and-chromium apartment. He'd had a lacquered Chinese cabinet especially made to hide his phone in and was always threatening to have it taken out of the house entirely. What would he do if I turned up bristling with wires and receivers and transmitters and batteries? Would he have a lacquered Chinese cabinet especially made to hide me in? Or would he have me taken out of the house entirely?

"Don't think I don't know how you feel," Dr. Graystone was saying. "It's a shocking and humiliating idea, especially for a woman as young as you are — the idea of putting on a hearing aid and wearing it. I'm not suggesting it lightly. But I wish you'd consider it — now, while you're young and pretty and happy and professionally successful — before impaired hearing has done your personality any harm. You're unusually sensitive — imaginative — highly strung. You want a lot from life. You've never accepted or admitted your handicap, even to yourself. So far you seem to have gotten away with it. But you can't get away with it forever. You'll find yourself in an emotional tailspin one of these days."

He was such a kind, fussy little old man. I was tempted to tell him that he needn't worry, that there'd be no tailspin, that Dr. Dettridge was curing me. But I didn't. I had a good idea what his opinion of Dr. Dettridge and his finger manipulations would be. He'd dismiss Dr. Dettridge as a high-priced charlatan. Well, what of it? If Dr. Dettridge could restore my hearing, what difference did it make what Dr. Graystone thought of him?

137

Dr. Graystone didn't know much about progressive deafness; he admitted it frankly. Well, then. Maybe Dr. Dettridge knew something about it. Maybe. Maybe. . .

"I wish you'd at least go into one of the hearing-aid companies and try an instrument."

Dr. Graystone was beginning to bore me. He was beginning to set my teeth on edge.

"I'll die first." I laughed shortly.

"Maybe you will," he said. "Maybe you'll die first."

In Dr. Bingle's syndicated newspaper health column — the same one in which I'd read about quinine years before — I read that a drop of iodine taken daily in a glass of water perked up dull ears. I tried that, for luck. I had my wisdom teeth out, for luck. I had body massage to improve my circulation (I'd read that poor circulation affected the hearing) and a course of ultraviolet-ray treatments for my sinuses. When I finished ultraviolet I had a series of cold shots — a new kind, just on the market. After that I had a complete gland check-up, for luck. I had read that glandular imbalance could affect hearing.

Was I never going to get my hearing restored? Dr. Dettridge still said he could do it, though it was taking even longer than he had anticipated, because I had so many colds. It had been eight months, now. My cure would probably take about a year, and about five hundred dollars more.

Dr. Graystone operated on my sinuses and sent me to Florida for a month of sun. In Florida I came across a book called *How to Breathe*. Shades of Anna Mary Dodge and *How to Drink Wine*. Shades of Mike Goodfriend and *How to Listen to Opera*. Deep breathing, according to *How to Breathe*, could cure anything. I faithfully practiced all the breathing exercises, facing east and repeating: "I am whole, I am powerful, I am strong, I am perfect" seven times, as the book instructed. It seemed as if this were where I had come in, as if I were six again, under the lilac bushes with my eyes closed and my fingers in my ears.

Was I never going to get my hearing restored?

In Florida I read a magazine article about a New York doctor whose treatment of phlebitis, by application of leeches to the jugular vein, was unexpectedly improving the hearing of some of his deaf patients. I hurried home and took the leech treatment.

"Now you'll never need to worry," Dr. Phlebitis told me, when I had spent a day and a hundred dollars at his private hospital with four leeches on each side of my neck. "As long as you live you'll never have phlebitis."

"What?" I said. Nothing had happened. My hearing felt as usual.

"I'm not sure I can cure you," Dr. Dettridge told me finally, when I'd been going to him for more than a year. "You have the kind of deafness that doesn't always respond to my treatment."

"When are you going to marry me?" Phil asked.

"Hadn't you better take lip-reading lessons and get a hearing aid? Don't put it off too long," Dr. Graystone urged.

Don't put it off too long. . . . Faintly, from Boston, from college years, I could hear dear old Dr. Richardson's voice. . . Don't put it off too long. . . I'd thought he was telling me not to put off marriage too long. . . . Funny thing about the hard-of-hearing, Dr. Richardson had said. . . Believe in miracles, all of them. . . Most stubborn and gullible people in the world. . . Try anything from first-rate otologists to high-priced charlatans to hocus-pocus and mail-order quackery. . . Won't stop believing in miracles till they go broke or die.

Miracles happen, I had assured him. . . .

But no miracle had happened. No miracle was going to happen.

Phil said, "Look, Junior, when are you going to marry me?"

"*Deaf?*" inquired a small advertisement hidden in the lower right-hand corner of the back page of the magazine section of my newspaper one Sunday morning. "You don't need to be deaf."

All I needed to do, the advertisement said, was send one dollar to a P. O. Box in Pennsylvania. By return mail I would receive a bottle of ear oil and a pair of small, invisible metal eardrums with which I would be able to hear perfectly.

I was tired and low-spirited. I had no business being low. I should have been on top of the world. My Wilcox pieces had developed into a *New Yorker* series. My second long article had been published in *Scribner's*, and Franklin P. Adams had noticed it. He had telephoned to congratulate me. He had quoted a paragraph from my article in his column.

To celebrate my success, Phil had taken me to the Coq d'Or on Fifty-second Street the night before. He had invited Charlie and Margaret Stone to help celebrate, but eighteen-month-old Chip was running a slight temperature, and Margaret didn't want to leave him. So Charlie came alone and Phil asked Ellen Pringle to make a fourth.

At the Coq d'Or every third person was a celebrity. I hoped to goodness I looked like a celebrity. I felt like one. I had on Le Dragon. I had felt like wearing it. I always felt good in it and it was still as gorgeous as ever, with its glittering coils of green beadwork and red fangs and ruby eye.

Phil had brought bootleg gin and Charlie suggested ginger-ale set-ups in memory of the old days in Hartfield. We talked about the old days when it had been the three of us together in Hartfield, hanging over the bridge railing in the blue twilight, watching the evening sky darken, watching the town lights thicken, full of ourselves, full of what we wanted.

Charlie raised his glass and smiled at me. He said something or other. . . Here's luck. . . Here's to you. . . something or other. . . My sweet and maddening Lazydog Charlie. He still wore the square blond mustache he had grown when he first came to New York. He still wouldn't take the trouble to speak up.

Phil raised his glass. "You're all set now, Junior," he said, smiling. "You always said you wanted to be a writer. Well — you're set."

Ellen Pringle raised her glass and smiled, too. She was stunning, as always — her tall, lithe figure sculptured in Maggie Rafferty white satin. She and I were good friends. Naturally we were wary of each other, because we both wanted Phil. But we were good friends.

She said it was fascinating about Adams. At least, I thought she did. I took it for granted that she meant it was fascinating about F.P.A.'s having telephoned to congratulate me on my *Scribner's* article. She certainly said it was fascinating about something. She had a well-placed voice and good Eastern finishing-school diction. I usually heard what she said.

Yes — the call from F.P.A. was definitely the big moment of my life so far, I answered with a laugh. I'd been so flustered when the phone rang and a voice said, "This is Adams of the *World*" that at first I hadn't registered. I'd thought it was just some plain, ordinary Mr. Adams. . . just some plain. . . ordinary. . .

I trailed my sentence vaguely, realizing from Ellen's face that I'd misheard her and was talking on the wrong track. What had she said? My heart skittered. It had sounded like fascinating about Adams. . . . Fascinating about adams, badams, wrinkle-lawraddams. . . . Often, if I thought a minute, it would flash over me what really had been said.

I looked at Phil, hoping for a clue, and saw him exchange amused glances with Ellen. Ellen cleared her throat slightly. Luckily the orchestra began playing just then and Charlie asked me to dance. As we moved across the floor I could see that Phil and Ellen were still smiling at each other, still amused about something. What was it? Were they amused about me?

They probably were. They probably thought I couldn't talk about anything except F.P.A. — that being quoted in "The Conning Tower" had gone to the little girl's head a mite. That I couldn't let anybody else talk about anything except me and my split-second of fame. That was probably what they were amused about. Oh, well. Let them think I was swell-headed. Just so they didn't think I hadn't heard.

Above the clamour of the music, Charlie was telling me about young Chip. The kid was always grabbing for pencils, trying to chew them up. Easy to see he was going to be literary, Charlie said with a grin.

I couldn't get my mind off Phil and Ellen. They were dancing together now — equally tall, equally stunning. They reminded me of something. It was the two Honorables, that week end in Devonshire. Rex Miller and Emily Trent. That was what Phil and Ellen reminded me of. Phil and Ellen matched, as Rex and Emily had matched. Phil was dark and Ellen was blond, yet they matched the way two cousins sometimes match; the way a brother and sister sometimes match. They seemed to share some bond, some special relationship, some conspiracy.

What were they so amused about? Me? Perhaps. Did it really matter? No — but I couldn't get it out of my mind. Had those two discovered that I was hard of hearing? Had they? Was that what they were amused about? The thought turned my heart cold with fear. Did they know? Had they talked about it together, perhaps? Laughed about it? Been amused at my expense? At my mistakes?

My mind swam with rage. Had they laughed at me behind my back — often, perhaps? Had they dared to do that? No one could laugh at me. . . No one. . . No tall, straight, beautiful woman could laugh at me. . . I'd die. . . I'd die of rage. . . of shame. . . The earth would open and swallow me. . . .

Back at the table again, Phil pulled me down beside him.

"When are you going to marry me?"

He asked me all the time nowadays, wherever we were.

I felt confused and light-headed. Did Phil know? Did Ellen know? She might. Had she told Phil? If she hadn't, she probably would sometime. That would be the end.

An important man like Phil wouldn't want me around, once he'd discovered I had something permanently the matter with me. That was why I had to have my hearing restored. But I wasn't going to have my hearing restored. I had tried everything. There wasn't going to be a miracle.

I felt weak and sick — panicky, as a child feels who wakes up suddenly to find itself alone, left alone in a big, still, frightening, empty room — empty, yet full — full of emptiness, darkness, silence. . . .

I began to cry.

Phil gave my ear an affectionate pinch.

"Going to marry me for Christmas, Junior? Or for my birthday? Or for Fourth of July?"

"Nope."

I shook my head. I could hardly speak. I was crying. Phil didn't know I was crying. There were no tears in my eyes. But

I was crying. The tears were falling deep down inside my heart.

"Deaf?" inquired the small advertisement hidden in the lower right-hand corner of the back page of the magazine section of my Sunday paper. "You don't need to be deaf."

All I needed to do was send one dollar to a P .O. Box in Pennsylvania. By return mail I would receive a bottle of ear oil and a pair of small, invisible metal eardrums to insert in my ears. When I had inserted these invisible eardrums in my ears I would be . . . invisible? Certainly not. With the small eardrums invisibly in my ears I would be able to hear perfectly.

Praise be. I wanted to be able to hear perfectly. I'd send one dollar to the P. O. Box in Pennsylvania immediately, I decided. Should I first write a pretty little letter to Judge Hopkins at the St. Louis Trust Company, asking for permission? I thought not. The Judge would want me to have perfect hearing. He would want me to be as quick and clever as my sisters — to be the best one in the family, not the least one. The Judge would agree — judicially, as a judge should — that under the circumstances one dollar was not one cent too much.

I'd send one dollar to Pennsylvania, just as I had once sent one dollar to a P. O. Box in Kansas and received by return mail an official Certificate of Newspaper Credentials bearing my full name and address, together with printed instructions that I was entitled everywhere to all courtesies customarily extended to the Press. This time I would receive by return mail a bottle of ear oil and a pair of small, invisible metal eardrums. Undoubtedly I would also receive an official Certificate of Hearing Credentials. Bearing my full name and address. Bearing printed instructions that I was entitled everywhere to all courtesies customarily extended to people with perfect hearing.

"Deaf?"

Not me. Not on your life. I didn't need to be deaf.

The Sunday magazine section slid to the floor. The next time my eye fell on the advertisement in the lower right-hand corner it inquired:

"Dead?"

I began to laugh. The two words always looked alike to me. I was always getting them mixed up.

"Deaf? Dead?"

"I bet you're deaf," my sister Ann had said, jeering, swinging her shiny black braids and spinning around on her heels. "I bet you're deaf. I bet you're dead. I bet you're deaf."

Which was it? Deaf or dead? Dead or deaf? They looked alike. Deaf or dead? Make up your mind. . . Which was it?. . . Was I getting hysterical over a silly newspaper ad?

"You don't need to be *deaf — dead.*" Not if you'll send one dollar to a P. O. Box. Not if you'll say "wrinkelstiltskin" seven times. Not if you'll have your adenoids out. Not if you'll take iron and have your tonsils out and stop having colds. Not if you'll be a dear, sweet, lovely child and say your prayers. Not if you'll take quinine and get your spinal cord humming. Not if you'll go to Richardson in Boston and Leopold in Vienna. Not if you'll take non-refillable capsules and have finger manipulations that have cured royalty. Not if you'll take calcium, iodine, ultraviolet, cold shots, vitamins, osteopathy, deep-breathing exercises, and leeches. Not if you'll stand up straight and stop eating so much fudge. Not if you'll brush your hair a hundred strokes and walk fifteen minutes with a book on your head. Not if you'll behave yourself and take no chances with your miracle. Not if you'll use broad a's and say eyether instead of eether. Not if you'll tie a new-minted penny to the tail of a kite and send it to a P. O. Box at the edge of the moon addressed to Santa Claus.

I leaned back in my chair, looking up at the ceiling, and

laughed and laughed. The room spun around. What was this — an emotional tailspin? Was this the emotional tailspin Dr. Graystone had warned me about?

Hurray for Dr. Graystone. The little man wanted to rig me up in a hearing aid, did he? He wanted to strap a battery on my leg, hide wires and a receiver under my hair, shove a transmitter down the front of me — make me into a mechanical monster, did he? He wanted to humiliate me, did he? While I was still young. Before my personality had been damaged. I'd die first. He wanted me to face reality, did he? That snag-toothed hag? Far better to face the ceiling. Far better to die and face the ceiling. "It is a far, far better thing that I do, than I have ever done. . ."

I found the exact center of the ceiling and drove in an invisible staple, tossing an invisible rope ladder through the staple, festooning it over the tops of light fixtures and curtain poles. I swung unconcernedly back and forth. I felt like Wrinkel. In fact, I was Wrinkel. Being Wrinkel was exciting — and perfectly safe, because you were invisible and inaudible. That was the fun of it.

"Deaf dead?"

What was the difference? The two words were alike. A person who was deaf might just as well be dead. Aunt Harriet said so. That was why I up and killed off Old Mr. Bascomb, standing at the gateway of the Old Soldiers' Home on that Memorial Day afternoon so long ago.

A person who was deaf might just as well be. . . deaf. . . dead. . . deaf was horrible. . . dead was horrible. . . horrible. . .

"What?" I said.

"What?" was perilous.

146

I laughed. I felt the way a little boy like Wrinkel would feel — strong and brave and full of secret glee. "What's the matter?" I taunted. "Something the matter?" I jeered, spinning around and around. *"What's the matter — cotton in your ears?"*

I was dead. I had killed myself off with the Seven Deadly Words. I was wearing my lovely pink organdy wedding dress and carrying a book called *How to Cope with Intermissions*.

Mr. and Mrs. Charles Stone met my boat. Margaret was tall and stunning, very sure of herself, devoted to her darling boy. "D'you ride?" she snapped, clearing her throat pointedly.

"Mock-seriously," I confessed, "in the high-pitched manner of Mr. Wilcox, as dear, sweet, and lovely a little man as you could find to wear in your buttonhole." I kept typing "Mr. and Mrs. Princeton Peebles" over and over so Aunt May and Aunt Harriet would think I had the making of a humorous writer.

Margaret was furious. She looked like nauseous Victorine Parry summoning me in from the train observation platform where Mike Goodfriend sat during an electrical storm holding a pair of shears. . . shoes. . . shears. . . whichever he preferred. She said I'd nevah be clevah; I was babyish and immatuah, veddy sweet for a child of fifteen, but I was always getting fifteen and fifty mixed up, was I not? She said I'd never marry a young man from a fine family like Cecil Holmes unless I washed my ears seven times every Saturday at eleven o'clock at Wrinkelmayer's with little sandwiches.

I was tickled she thought I was dangerous. "Restez-vous," I drawled. It was an expression I'd picked up dirt-cheap and smuggled in. "Whoa, Wrinkelpuss," I said. "Who's so Honorable?" I was cast as an Indian princess in the school pageant,

147

so I scalped the hat with the Red and Yellow Cuckoo on it right off her head. Like Jim Fisher, she was mighty sensitive about getting bald. She lay in her coffin, looking as French as possible in pink and powder blue, a milk-glass hen, with sequins. Everyone said she was wonderful; she'd been reading lips unconsciously most of her life. Judas Priest, was she deaf or dead?

I'd like my old friend Pamela Jones, Charlie told me. She was a good sort, married to that nice young architect, devoted to her darling little boy.

"Yes and No, Wrinkelprune," I told him, swinging my gate back and forth, hoping against hope he'd wrinkelask me to the wrinkeldance.

He said, "By the way, Honey — do I imagine it or do you have a little trouble with your hearing?"

"Oh, dryopteris!"

"Glubglubglubglub?" he asked. My sweet and maddening Slow Coach Charlie.

"Cut your throat and drown yourself vite, vite, vite!" I shouted. Rochefoucauld snored securely on his towel, contented with pink and yellow bonbons. He was always much quicker to comprehend than I was.

"I say, the feller died, y'know!" It was Dr. Abraham Leopold.

Waving his editorial blue pencil at the pier was the Honorable Phil Braley.

There were two of him — Ring Once and Ring Twice. Ring Once was for me — a nice, big, rumble-throated man who took a big turnip watch from his pocket and said All right. . . She hears all right if she listens. . . She'll outgrow it. . . in a voice I could hear clear across the city room of the *Hartfield Register* without trying. Ring Twice was for Ellen Pringle. Snow Princess Ellen was used to having two of everything.

Ring Twice wore really good herringbone tweed and drank rather a lot. "Dead?" he exclaimed. "Ridiculous! Skip it. Hey? What say?" He got my spinal cord humming and stood me on the threshold of the royal box at the Opera, facing east in yards of beautiful silk. It was a lacquer box, especially made by Alexander Graham Bell to ship his wife as a missionary to China. She was a wonderful woman — very dead. She and I would make a dandy pair of mantelpiece ornaments. There were newspaper clippings to prove it: *The Case of a Couple of Cold Clods*, by Michael West.

"Better face reality," I said.

Ring Twice looked at me through half-closed eyes and took a long pull from his whisky and soda. " 'It is a far, far better thing that I do. . .' That's Sidney Carton in *A Tale of Two Cities*, Junior. Not *Héloïse and Abélard*," he scolded. He despised mistakes and didn't think much of women, either.

Ring Once tipped up my chin and kissed me. He was such a nice man. "How do you like that, Miss Cotton Ears?" he asked. "Ever think of discovering electricity?"

"I'll die first!"

I laughed, swinging unconcernedly on my rope ladder, swinging out of my living-room window, hurtling through the air. It was exciting and perfectly safe. Poison, the apartment-house doorman, was on duty down below — gorgeous in white gloves and military chin-strap and mulberry-colored livery decked out in gold braid. He caught me in mid-air as I fell. Caught me easily — in one of his huge, white-gloved hands. Nuttin to it. He did it outa tha goodness of his heart.

"Gotta watch out fa dese deef people," he told the crowd that collected on Washington Square. "Get low in dere minds, see. One'll swallow persen — annudder'll jump outa tha winda — annudder'll go off in a trance, like, and sit fa hours staring

149

at tha ceiling. They're all tha same. I know. My Old Man's deef. I can spot 'em."

I was dead the next day, when I went to a hearing-aid company and bought myself an electric hearing aid. I was hardly conscious of the dim, funereal reception room and of the middle-aged receptionist, who spoke distinctly, shaping her words with her lips, accustomed to talking to dead people.

I was hardly conscious of the salesman in the inner office who tested my hearing and handed me a small round receiver.

"Hold that to your ear," he directed, adjusting the battery and transmitter lying on the table between us. "Now I am speaking in a very low voice. Can you hear what I'm saying?"

I nodded. I could hear him. . . "Can you hear now?" my sister Ann had asked, when I was seven and had had my adenoids out. "Can you hear perfectly?"

"Now I'm going to turn my back to you — so you won't read my lips — and say numbers in a very low voice," the salesman told me. "Ninety-nine. Thirty-five. Sixty-six."

"I hear it." I said, remembering the pale pink sea shell Mrs. George Furness brought Ann and me from the East marked "Souvenir of Rye Beach, New Hampshire.". . . "I hear it," I had told Ann excitedly, listening for the roaring sound of the ocean in the shell. "I hear it forever after!"

The salesman said, "Good. You're one of the lucky ones. Not everyone can get clear hearing with one of these gimmicks, you know. Different people get different results. It depends on the type and degree of hearing loss."

He was a pleasant, egg-shaped man. He reminded me of Allen Keith, the music critic on the *Hartfield Register*. I always felt that if you wound Keith up he would play and sing beautifully.

"You're one of the lucky ones," this Keith repeated, pleased with me, pleased with himself, wound up, playing and singing beautifully. "You'll be able to get the approximation of normal hearing with a hearing aid. After you've worn it a while and got accustomed to it, you'll be able to forget all about it. You'll be hearing the grass grow."

"Good," I said. "I've always wanted to hear the grass grow."

"You wear the receiver under your hair, you know," Keith played and sang, played and sang. "No one will know it's there. . . You wear it under your hair. . . You'll want to let your hair grow longer, of course. You won't want short hair any more. You might get a new permanent wave and a few artificial curls to cover the gimmick while you're waiting for your own hair to grow longer. Some of my customers have done that."

No one will know it's there. . .

You wear it under your hair. . . .

When Phil came to take me to dinner that evening I was dead.

He rumpled my hair, as he always did. Then — "What have we here, Junior?"

"A gimmick," I told him. This was the end. He'd send me away now. "You wear it under your hair," I said. Then you don't need to be deaf. . . You don't need to be deaf. . . You just need to be dead. . . .

He nodded at me approvingly. "Good girl. I've been wondering if you wouldn't get one of those, one of these days."

"You know that I'm hard of hearing?"

"Everybody who knows you knows that, Junior."

"Well, I'll be a sonofabitch!"

"And nobody gives a damn."

151

"Well, I'll be a son. . . of. . . a. . . Turn your back to me," I said to Phil. "Turn your back and say something in a very low voice. Say, Now is the time for all good men."

"All right." He turned his back. "Now is the time for all good men."

"Whisper something. Whisper, The quick brown fox. . ."

"All right. The quick brown fox jumps over the lazy dog."

"Whisper something else. Anything at all. Anything you want."

"When are you going to marry me?"

"You mean you really don't mind, Phil? You mean it's all right? It's okay?"

"When are you going to marry me?"

He was such a nice man. I married him.